Alan R. Moon

TICKET TO RIDE™
PUZZLE BOOK

Original Ticket to Ride art by Julien Dulval.

All other images © Shutterstock except the following:
Alamy: /Antiqua Print Gallery: 77C; /Bildagentur-online: 64-65; /Chronicle: 126BR, 129TR, 143B, 150-151, 178BL; /Classic Image: 21TL, 94B, 114-115; /colaimages: 105BKG; /Ian Dagnall Computing: 73C; / Glasshouse Images: 106BL, 124BL; /Patrick Guenette: 53B; /Heritage Image Partnership Ltd: 35B; /History and Art Collection: 167BKG; /ITAR-TASS News Agency: 160BL; /IllustratedHistory: 34BL; /imageBROKER: 53T, 148BL; /Imago Europe Collection: 92B; /Imago History Collection: 71T; /Interfoto: 34-35, 42-43, 60-61, 100R; /KGPA Ltd: 121BL; /Jeff Krotz: 132-133; /Lebrecht Music & Arts: 142B; /Nerthuz: 176-177; /Niday Picture Library: 46TR, 107B, 125BL; /North Wind Picture Archives: 24-25; /Matteo Omied: 161BL; /The Print Collector: 10BL, 39T; /Sergey Pykhonin: 108BKG; /Science History Images: 179BL, 186-187; /Meiji Showa: 168-169; / World History Archive: 89B, 139BKG

Every effort has been made to acknowledge correctly and contact the source and/or copyright holder of each picture any unintentional errors or omissions will be corrected in future editions of this book.

Special thanks to Adrien Martinot at Days of Wonder Studio, and to Danielle Robb at Asmodee Entertainment.

Published in 2021 by Welbeck
an imprint of Welbeck Non-Fiction Limited,
part of Welbeck Publishing Group
Based in London and Sydney.
www.welbeckpublishing.com

A CIP catalogue record for this book is available from the British Library

Design: Tall Tree Limited and Eliana Holder
Editorial: Chris Mitchell

ISBN 978-1-78739-598-5

Printed in Dubai

10 9 8 7 6 5 4 3 2

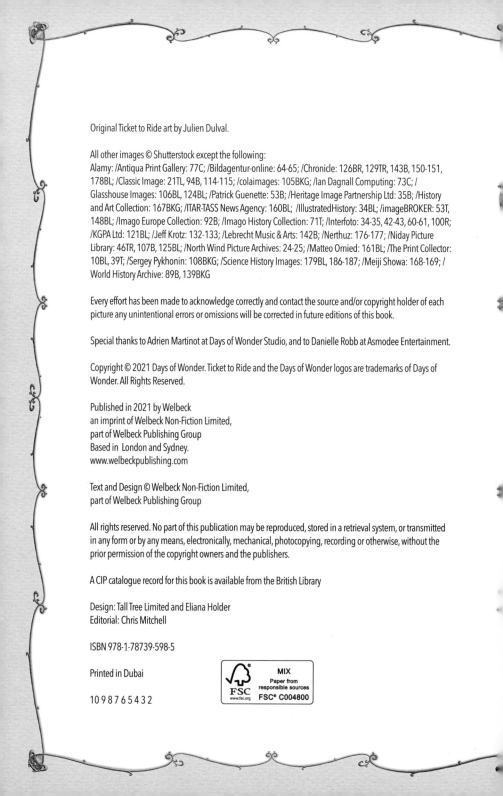

MIX
Paper from
responsible sources
FSC® C004800

Alan R. Moon

TICKET TO RIDE™
PUZZLE BOOK

TRAVEL THE WORLD WITH 100
OFF-THE-RAILS PUZZLES

**RICHARD
WOLFRIK GALLAND**

WELBECK

Contents

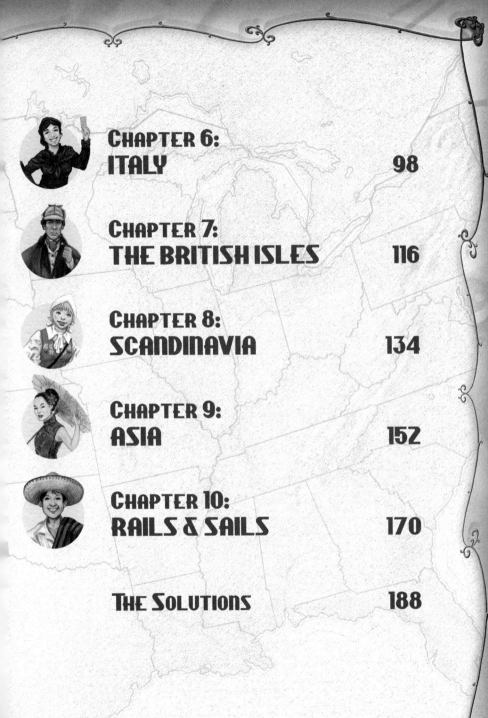

Introduction

Welcome to the *Ticket to Ride Puzzle Book*! Whether you are an expert at the board game or a complete *Ticket to Ride* novice, there is plenty to be enjoyed in this challenging around-the-world puzzle adventure. You do not need any knowledge of the rules and tactics of the board game to enjoy the riddles and puzzles in this book, although the location solutions for each of the "Discover..." puzzles can be found on each game board of the appropriate *Ticket to Ride* edition, if you need a hint.

It is the year 1900 and you are a young tourist about to set off on a tour of the world. Travelling by rail (and occasionally boat and bicycle), you will experience the sights and sounds of the turn of the century. As you journey, you will encounter 100 conundrums and riddles related to the places you visit and the people you meet.

If you would like to dip in and out of the book, solving puzzles as you go, then there is plenty to be enjoyed. Have fun! However, the book can also be "played" and "completed" for those looking for a more rigorous challenge.

Each puzzle will reward you with one or more train cards – and sometimes there is a bonus for completing the puzzle within a certain time limit. Just as in the original game, there are a variety of colours of train cards to be won: black, blue, green, orange, purple, red, white, yellow and multi-coloured. Keep track of the number of each colour of train cards you obtain as you progress.

The aim is to collect as many of each colour as you can. Depending on what type of puzzler you are – for example, whether you are better at visual, linguistic or logical puzzles – you may find some colours are easier to collect than others. This is where the multi-coloured train cards are invaluable. They are "wildcards" and can count as any colour that you need more of. When you have finished the book, compare your final tally to the table opposite. How do you rate as a globe-trotting puzzle-solver?

NUMBER OF CARDS	RESULT
0-3 of every colour	First-time adventurer
4-7 of every colour	Sightseer in training
8-11 of every colour	Trendy tourist
12-15 of every colour	First-class explorer
16-19 of every colour	Modern-day Magellan
20+ of every colour	Ticket to Ride champion

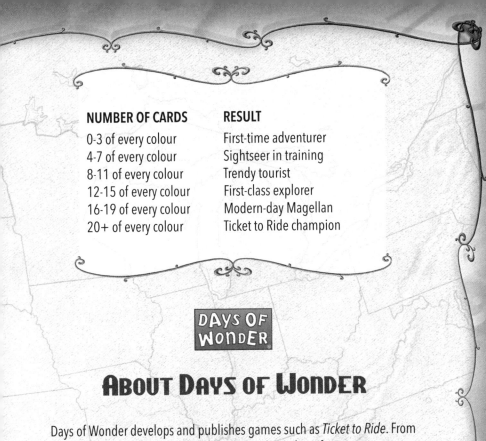

DAYS OF WONDER

ABOUT DAYS OF WONDER

Days of Wonder develops and publishes games such as *Ticket to Ride*. From its insistence on releasing only a very limited number of new games, to its uncompromising board game production values and unique in-house digital development team, Days of Wonder has consistently raised the bar with an unmatched string of hits that includes: *Ticket to Ride*, the world's best-selling train game; *Small World*, the legendary fantasy game of epic conquests; and *Memoir '44*, the World War II saga with 20 expansions to its credit.

The *Ticket to Ride* board game, designed by Alan R. Moon, was first published in 2004 and won the world's most prestigious game award, the German *Spiel des Jahres*, in the same year. It has now sold over 12 million copies in more than 40 different languages, making it a truly global phenomenon.

NORTH AMERICA

Evidence suggests that settlers from Central Asia were the first to populate North America more than 14,000 years ago. The first European to set foot on the continent was probably the Norse explorer Leif Erikson around 1000 CE. It would be almost another five centuries before two other Europeans, Christopher Columbus and John Cabot, independently "discovered" the Americas, thanks to their limited awareness of world geography.

The exploits of these explorers gave rise to a tide of colonization, some brutal wars and the foundation of the United States and Canada. During the second half of the nineteenth century, railroads played a significant role in the more peaceful development of these nations, linking the Atlantic East Coast to the Pacific West and the treasure troves of natural resources in between.

Your journey begins way out west!

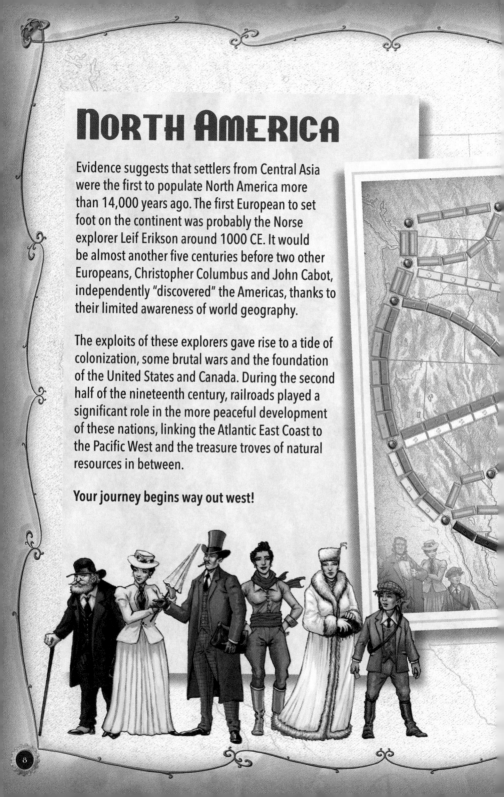

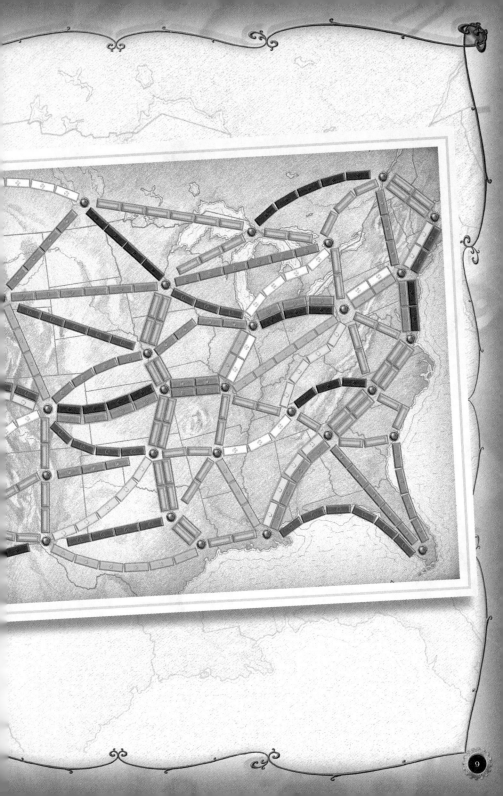

DISCOVER NORTH AMERICA

It's the year 1900, and an auspicious time to begin your travels. You have decided to start from a city almost as far west as they come, and you settle down in a local coffee shop to begin plotting your route.

Glancing down at your map, you spot your first – of very few, you hope – impediments to your journey. You had traded your last pair of good socks (with no holes!) for it with an old gold miner, and you feel like he got by far the better of the deal, because almost none of the place names are legible.

The names of 36 North American cities are concealed in the grid opposite. They may run horizontally, vertically, diagonally, forwards or backwards.

To make things more challenging, you must work out which cities are included by matching them with the facts below.

1.   Terminus of the W&A line, named by rail engineer J. Edgar Thomson.   A_____
2.   Location of America's first lighthouse (built in 1716).   B_____
3.   Known as "Stampede City" after its world-famous rodeo.   C_____
4.   Capital of the Mountain State.   C_____
5.   Host of the World's Columbian Exposition in 1893.   C_____
6.   Location of the State Fair of Texas since 1886.   D_____
7.   Famously situated exactly one mile above sea level.   D_____
8.   Location of the Great Lakes Aquarium.   D_____
9.   Known as the "Six Shooter Capital" in the 1880s.   E_ _____
10. Briefly home of the world's largest indoor swimming pool in the late 1800s.   H_____
11. The world's first domed stadium was built here.   H_____
12. Known as the "Paris of the Plains" during the 1920-33 prohibition.   K_____ ____
13. The "Marriage Capital of the World" since the 1930s.   L__ _____
14. Named after a stone outcropping on the banks of the Arkansas River.   L_____ ____
15. Home of a famous hillside sign and landmark.   L__ _____
16. City founded by Julia Tuttle in 1896.   M____
17. Home of Saint Joseph's Oratory, Canada's largest church.   M_____
18. Known as "The Athens of the South" and "Music City".   N_____
19. Sold to the United States by Napoléon Bonaparte in 1803.   N__ _____
20. The first capital of the US under the Constitution of the United States.   N__ ____
21. Location of the world's first parking meter in the 1930s.   O_____ _____
22. Purported birthplace of the Reuben sandwich.   O____
23. Named after a mythical self-resurrecting creature.   P_____
24. Known as the "Steel City" and the "City of Bridges".   P_____
25. The city's name was decided by a coin toss (vs. "Boston").   P_____
26. Named after a famous English Elizabethan explorer.   R_____

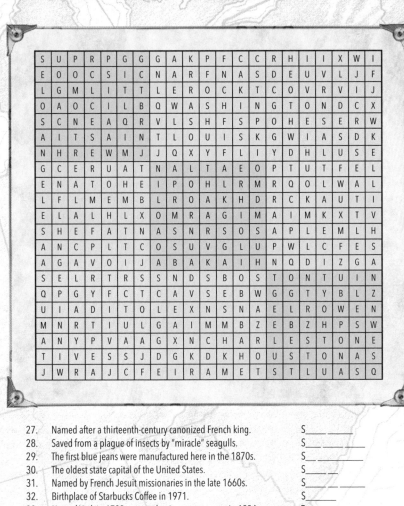

```
S U P R P G G G A K P F C C R H I I X W I
E O O C S I C N A R F N A S D E U V L J F
L G M L I T T L E R O C K T C O V R V I J
O A O C I L B Q W A S H I N G T O N D C X
S C N E A Q R V L S H F S P O H E S E R W
A I T S A I N T L O U I S K G W I A S D K
N H R E W M J J Q X Y F L I Y D H L U S E
G C E R U A T N A L T A E O P T U T F E L
E N A T O H E I P O H L R M R Q O O L W A L
L F L M E M B L R O A K H D R C K A U T I
E L A L H L X O M R A G I M A I M K X T V
S H E F A T N A S N R S O S A P L E M L H
A N C P L T C O S U V G L U P W L C F E S
A G A V O I J A B A K A I H N Q D I Z G A
S E L R T R S S N D S B O S T O N T U I N
Q P G Y F C T C A V S E B W G G T Y B L Z
U I A D I T O L E X N S N A E L R O W E N
M N R T I U L G A I M M B Z E B Z H P S W
A N Y P V A A G X N C H A R L E S T O N E
T I V E S S J D G K D K H O U S T O N A S
J W R A J C F E I R A M E T S T L U A S Q
```

27. Named after a thirteenth-century canonized French king.   S____ _____

28. Saved from a plague of insects by "miracle" seagulls.   S____ ____ _____

29. The first blue jeans were manufactured here in the 1870s.   S__ _____

30. The oldest state capital of the United States.   S_____ __

31. Named by French Jesuit missionaries in the late 1660s.   S_____ __ _____

32. Birthplace of Starbucks Coffee in 1971.   S_____

33. Named York in 1793; reverted to its current name in 1834.   T_____

34. Birthplace of Greenpeace in 1971.   V_____

35. Home to more than 175 embassies of foreign nations.   W_____ __

36. Named after the Cree word for "muddy water".   W_____

REWARD
You win two yellow train cards for correctly identifying and finding half of all of the cities and another two if you find them all.

FOR SOLUTION SEE PAGE 190

MAKE TRACKS

Settling into your seat, you can feel the anticipation and excitement that comes with a new journey rising within you. You look around the carriage and count yourself extremely lucky to be travelling in such comfort.

Some of the original pioneers established settlements before the railroads arrived to connect them to civilization, and back then it could take as long as five months to cross the country! Modern engineering is truly a wonderful thing, you think, as a jolt on the track nearly knocks you from your seat.

Can you design a railroad that connects every station and township?

Draw a single continuous line around the grid that passes through all the stations and townships.

If the line enters a station, turn left or right within its square before passing straight through the next square you come to. Ensure that this works for both routes going in and out of the station.

If the line enters a township, keep going straight through its square before turning left or right in the next square. Ensure that this works for at least one route going into the township.

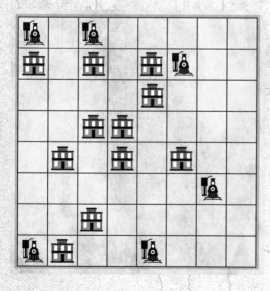

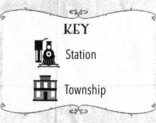

FOR SOLUTION SEE PAGE 190

REWARD
Successfully connect the stations and townships to win two orange train cards.

Spare a Dime?

In your travels you have noticed that entertainers tend to gather together in certain cities that then become hot-spots of creativity. One such up-and-coming place is Los Angeles. Most people know it as the country's largest oil-producing city, but it has started attracting performers of all types ever since the first movie was shot there a few years ago in 1897.

You pass buskers, dancers and street magicians all putting in performances that you would be lucky to see on stage at most town theatres. You soon notice something unusual: an especially large crowd all laughing and hollering, and you excitedly rush over to investigate.

An old man, well-dressed but somewhat unkempt, is shaking a can of coins. He is surrounded by a crowd of people who appear to waving dollar bills, throwing coins and laughing. Two police officers are watching from the sidelines, shaking their heads and smiling. You ask them what is going on – it doesn't seem like any other act that you have witnessed that day.

"That's Dougie Dimes, he's well known around here – an old oil worker. If you offer him a dollar and a dime, he takes the dime, every time. Even with everything else to see, tourists love him. Poor guy."

Just at that moment, Dougie turns his attention to you. "Excuse me, can you spare a dime?" he asks good-naturedly.

You start to hand over a 10-cent coin but, feeling generous and curious to see what happens, you decide to give him your last dollar bill instead. Just as the policeman said, the old man ignores the note and accepts the coin with a grin.

You turn back to the police officers, bewildered. "But that doesn't make any sense. Is the fellow all right?"

"Yes," says the other officer. "He's probably the smartest one out here."

Why would the officer make such a judgement?

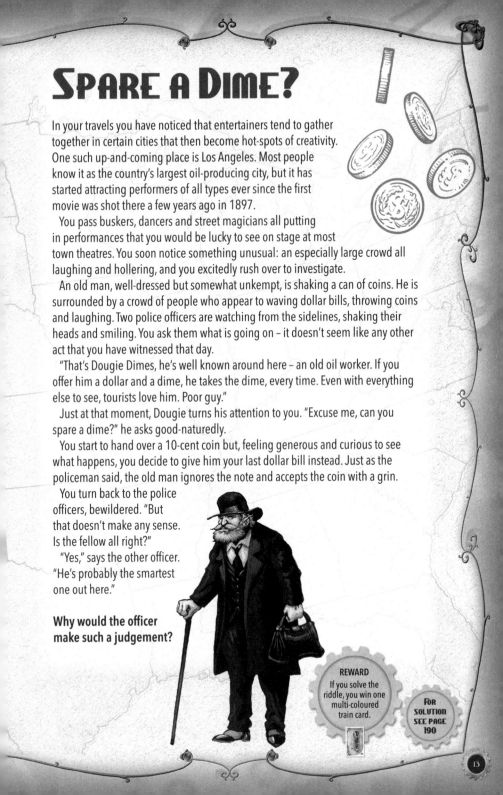

REWARD
If you solve the riddle, you win one multi-coloured train card.

FOR SOLUTION SEE PAGE 190

THE PIONEERS

Your next rail journey takes you through the Old West on the trail of the first pioneers. It is a long journey, and it is only natural that you get talking with the others sharing the carriage with you. It is one of the great pleasures of long-distance travel that you get the chance to meet all manner of people.

One fellow passenger by the name of Brake is of particular interest, and you spend many enjoyable hours learning of his life. He reveals himself to be the scion of one of the families who made their fortune out here in the 1890s.

Mr Brake talks about his own kin and four other successful families with obvious admiration. Unfortunately, he has a wandering conversational style, which makes it hard to piece together the facts: in other words, which family set up which business, where and in what year.

Good manners compel you to listen rather than seek clarification.

Can you fill in all the facts about the five families from the following snippets?

"My family set up in Carson City sometime before the Grahams started preaching and the McDonalds established their business."

"The steelworks started running in 1892 but not out of Sacramento or Denver."

"Neither the Harvey family, who started their business in 1891, nor the Steins ran the farms in Boise."

"The business in Fresno was established in 1893. The hotels were not yet open in 1890."

"The mines were not set up in Denver."

Family	Year Est.	Business	Location
Stein			
Harvey			
Brake			
Graham			
McDonald			

	1894	1893	1892	1891	1890	Farming	Hotels	Mining	Preaching	Steel	Boise	Carson City	Denver	Fresno	Sacramento
Stein															
Harvey															
Brake															
Graham															
McDonald															
Boise															
Carson City															
Denver															
Fresno															
Sacramento															
Farming															
Hotels															
Mining															
Preaching															
Steel															

TIP: This is a classic logic puzzle, put a tick in a box when you have confirmed a piece of information and a cross in any of the boxes you know to be false. For example: if the Brakes set up in Carson City, put a tick in the box intersected by "Brake" and "Carson City" and put crosses in Brake/Boise, Brake/Denver, Brake/Fresno, Brake/Sacramento, Carson City/Stein, Carson City/Harvey, Carson City/Graham and Carson City/McDonald.

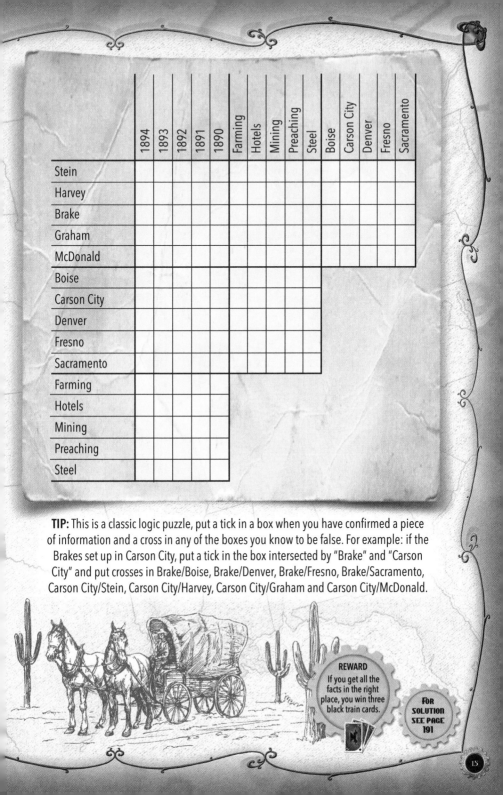

REWARD
If you get all the facts in the right place, you win three black train cards.

FOR SOLUTION SEE PAGE 191

CONNECT THE MIDWEST

You have just spent a very enjoyable handful of days in Denver, where you experienced a very different type of gold rush from that happening in other parts of the country – the Carnation Gold Rush. The flowers were almost everywhere you looked, giving the city a very cheerful façade indeed.

As you wait on the platform at Denver Union Station, clutching your bouquet of flowers, you think happily of the next stage of the journey, when you are due to meet your friend Eliza in Chicago. To pass the time as you wait, you turn to an amusing puzzle book given to you by a friendly train guard back in Seattle.

You must work out the route and insert the tracks into the grid below in the 10 minutes before the train arrives.

The numbers on the periphery tell you how many rail sections must be in that row or column.

You may place only a straight or a curved section inside a box. The tracks cannot cross themselves.

Straight

Curve

Can you connect Denver to Chicago?

The Colorado State Capitol in Denver, just finished and open to visitors.

The elevated "subway" train in Chicago looking north up Wabash Avenue.

FOR SOLUTION SEE PAGE 191

REWARD
If you find your way to your destination within 10 minutes, you win two white train cards. If it takes you longer than 10 minutes, you win one white train card.

CLAY'S PIGEON

Travelling on the Pennsylvania Railroad from Philadelphia to New York, you have the good fortune to make the acquaintance of Lucas Clay, the engine driver. He invites you into his cab, clearly glad of some human company.

A pigeon is perched on one of the pressure gauges, seemingly at home amid the noise and smoke.

"That's Betsy," says Lucas with obvious pride. "I'm training her to be a racer."

You wait for him to elaborate, and he is happy to oblige.

"We're on the home stretch now. My engine keeps a constant 40 miles per hour. When we pass the old chapel, we'll be exactly 100 miles from New York City and that's when I let Betsy fly.

"She'll head home, straight as an arrow at a steady 90 miles per hour until she reaches the station in NYC, then she'll fly straight back to me at the same speed. Yes, she'll keep going to-and-fro, non-stop, until we pull into the station!"

Lucas offers you a wide grin that breaks up his coal-speckled face. You can't be sure whether or not he's pulling your leg. But he asks you:

"How many miles will Betsy fly after I let her loose until she joins us at the station?"

REWARD
If you successfully solve Clay's riddle, you win a red train card.

FOR SOLUTION SEE PAGE 191

New York Minutes

Enjoying a bagel at a diner in Brooklyn, you overhear a heated debate coming from the next table.

Four brothers want to get to the field in time to watch the Superbas baseball game, which starts in just 19 minutes. Listening closer, it becomes clear that their normal mode of transport – their carriage – is under repairs. Something about the youngest brother's recklessness is mentioned, and he hurriedly changes the subject.

The only transport available is the eldest brother's horse, which is strong enough to take two of them at once, and make multiple trips.

Art is a youthful 15 years old, rides like a demon and can get to the ballpark in a minute. Bernie is 23 and can make the journey in 2 minutes. Charles is 30 and can do it in 5 minutes, while Donny, who is 42, takes a careful 10 minutes to get there.

They will clearly need to double up, but Donny insists that the eldest brother on the horse must be in charge. He looks sternly at Art when he says this.

The brothers will be leaving in exactly two minutes – giving 17 minutes to travel – and will need a strategy by then. How can all four brothers get to the field in time for the game?

REWARD
If you figure it out within two minutes, take two blue train cards. If you succeeded but took longer than two minutes, you win one blue train card.

FOR SOLUTION SEE PAGE 191

THE BIG APPLE

Dutch colonists founded the United States's most populous city (as New Amsterdam) in 1624, but it came under English rule 40 years later and was renamed, along with its surrounding state, after the Duke of York.

Shortly after your arrival, you walk down to the East River to get your bearings. Even for someone becoming as experienced at travel as you are, the hustle and bustle of New York can be quite overwhelming. And if you thought the river would be any different, you were wrong. Workers are swarming everywhere, and you find yourself buffeted in a tide of life whichever way you turn.

You stop a passing woman who seems a little less busy than the others and ask what they are all doing. She squints at you in surprise.

"Where are you from? Don't you know anything? It's only going to be the longest suspension bridge in the world when it's done with." She looks out over the river with pride. "The Williamsburg Bridge it's called. This is the finest city in the world." She whistles and hurries off before you can ask anything else, quickly enveloped by the crowds.

It's certainly a wonderful city, but the finest in the world? You have a lot of travelling to do before you can begin to judge that! However, there is certainly a lot to take in. Everywhere you look you find iconic sights and famous landmarks.

Can you unscramble the anagrams of 15 prominent 21st century locations in the city?

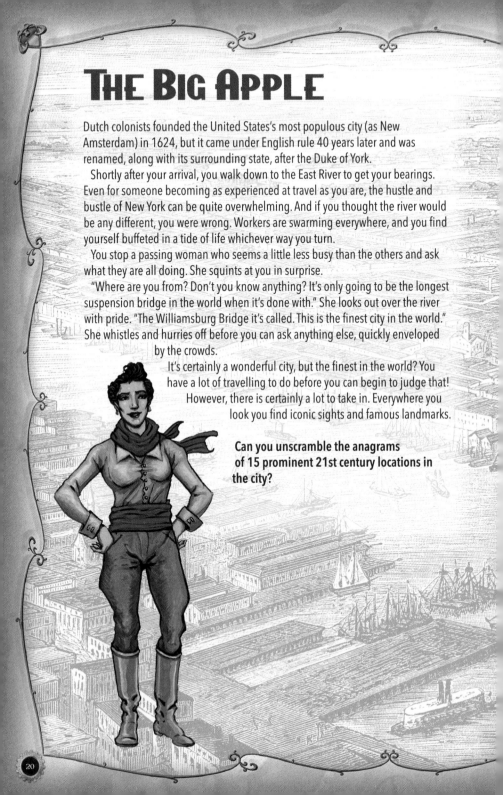

A modern view of New York.

1. YOLK BORN
2. LACK PARTNER
3. LEACHES
4. TWIN NACHO
5. SALIVATE GEL
6. INDIGESTIBLE TEMPURA
7. ARMY CRAG PERK
8. VIEW ACHING GELLER
9. LET NIL CONCERN
10. ISOLATED SEWER
11. TWO MINT DEWS
12. SHOO
13. REQUEST AIMS
14. SUNTAN EDITION
15. LAW LETTERS

REWARD
If you unscramble all the names, you win two purple train cards.

FOR SOLUTION SEE PAGE 192

YULETIDE

You arrive in Boston on the new Lake Shore Limited train
from New York. The views have been as fantastic as the name
suggested and your only complaint is that, as you travel further
north, the temperature has dropped considerably.

Your travelling companion for this leg of the trip has been one Mrs Blair,
a very glamorous woman who has happily shared her extensive knowledge of
the customs of Boston with you – but you rather wish she had spared her warm
and expensive fur coat with you instead.

As you pull in, the first snow starts to fall and as Mrs Blair had promised it
would be, the city was in full preparations for the winter festivities to begin.
In fact, as you gather your bearings, a goods train pulls into the station with a
dozen freight cars in tow. Each carriage is painted with a three-letter code.

**Two of the carriages are in the
wrong places, which ones?**

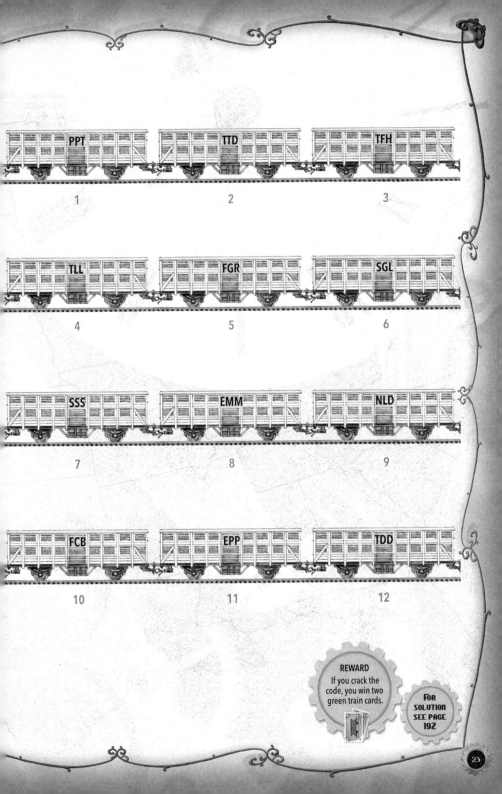

PPT
1

TTD
2

TFH
3

TLL
4

FGR
5

SGL
6

SSS
7

EMM
8

NLD
9

FCB
10

EPP
11

TDD
12

REWARD
If you crack the code, you win two green train cards.

FOR SOLUTION SEE PAGE 192

23

All Change!

It's been a long journey, spanning the entire continent. You have spent hundreds of hours on trains criss-crossing this young and hopeful nation, and while you are sad that it is almost over, if you're honest you can't wait to get home to put your feet up! For a little while, at least, because you are already excitedly planning your next adventure, which will take you overseas.

You return to New York, where you prepare to embark across the ocean. Before you leave you purchase two hand-made postcards showing the Brooklyn Bridge, the longest suspension bridge in the world – at least, until the Williamsburg Bridge is finished! They are not exactly the same, though.

How quickly can you find 12 differences between the picture on the left and the one on the right?

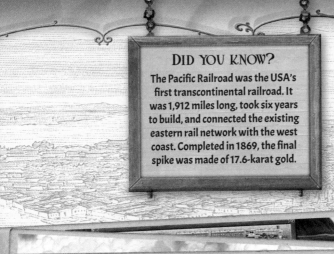

DID YOU KNOW?

The Pacific Railroad was the USA's first transcontinental railroad. It was 1,912 miles long, took six years to build, and connected the existing eastern rail network with the west coast. Completed in 1869, the final spike was made of 17.6-karat gold.

Brooklyn Bridge, towering over the East River, looking toward Manhattan.

REWARD

If you find all 12 differences within 10 minutes, you win two multi-coloured train cards. If you find them in longer than 10 minutes, you win two red train cards.

FOR SOLUTION SEE PAGE 192

EUROPE

The continent of Europe is situated in the north, western and eastern hemispheres, with Asia along its eastern border and the Atlantic Ocean along the west. It may be the second smallest continent (only Australia is smaller) but it has enjoyed thousands of years of human settlement. Its long history has seen the birth of Western Civilization, the Roman Empire, the Renaissance, the Enlightenment and the Industrial Revolution. In 1901 it is truly at the forefront of development, and you cannot wait to begin exploring the tapestry of nations and empires that make up this bustling and ever-changing continent.

Europe is a wonderful patchwork of cultures and you know that there is no better way to appreciate its rich diversity than a continental rail tour!

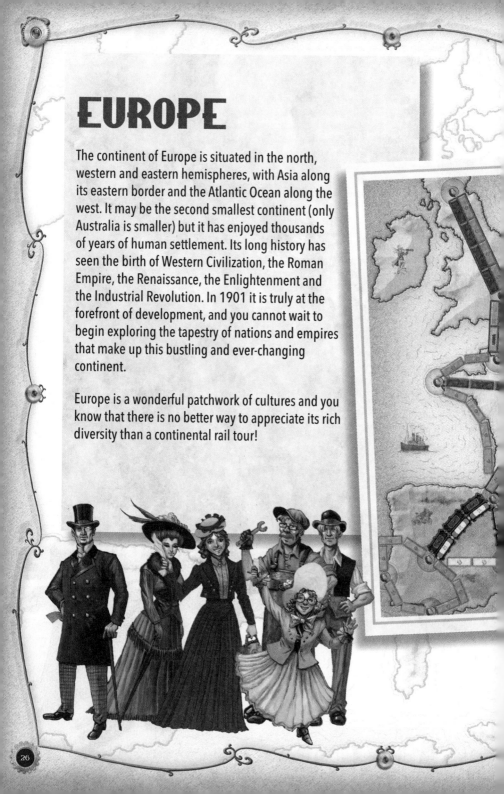

Discover Europe

Having sailed across the ocean, you are keen to continue your journey by your favoured medium – rail. You are in the Scottish city of Edinburgh and as you wander the hills of the Old Town you are enchanted by the sturdiness and age of the buildings, walls and even castle around you. The United States of America is still being built – it is exciting, fresh and full of opportunity, but it does not yet have the feeling of permanence and immovability that Edinburgh has.

After spending an enjoyable – if notably chilly – couple of days in the city, you head to Waverley Station where you take a seat under its new glass dome and begin charting your route through this unexplored continent. You aren't used to so many different languages on the map though…

The past and present names of 44 European cities (in a native language) are concealed in the grid opposite. They may run horizontally, vertically, diagonally, forwards or backwards. To make things more challenging, you must work out which cities are included by matching them with their facts below.

1.	Became capital after the fall of the Ottoman Empire, before name was changed to Ankara.	A_____
2.	The oldest European capital city.	A_____
3.	The capital of Catalonia.	B_____
4.	Home of the Académie de Marine (Royal Naval Academy).	B_____
5.	Once connected to Rome by the Via Appia (Appian Way).	B_____
6.	Famous for its statue of a little boy urinating.	B_____
7.	Site of Vlad the Impaler's princely fortress.	B_____
8.	Joined across the Danube by the Széchenyi Chain Bridge.	B_____
9.	Ancient Andalusian city settled around 1104 BCE.	C_____
10.	Was once known as Byzantium and later became Istanbul.	C_____
11.	Gdańsk was known by this name while under Prussian rule.	D_____
12.	Port on the Channel coast, famous for its scallop festival.	D_____
13.	Venue for the arts and comedy festival known as the Fringe.	E_____
14.	Main railway terminus in Eastern Anatolia.	E_____
15.	Annual host of SPIEL, the world's largest board games exposition.	E_____
16.	Birthplace of writer Johann Wolfgang von Goethe.	F_____
17.	The second largest city in Ukraine.	K_____
18.	Home of The Little Mermaid statue.	K_____
19.	Location of Arsenalna, the world's deepest metro station.	K_____
20.	Was known as Olisipo while part of the Roman Empire.	L_____
21.	Capital with enough trees to qualify as a forest as defined by the UN.	L_____
22.	Its coat of arms is a bear eating from a strawberry tree.	M_____
23.	Mediterranean port city and birthplace of bouillabaisse.	M_____
24.	Site of Saint Basil's Cathedral and the Kremlin.	M_____
25.	Annual host of Oktoberfest.	M_____
26.	The capital of Sicily.	P_____
27.	Famous for the nine-day Festival of San Fermín.	P_____

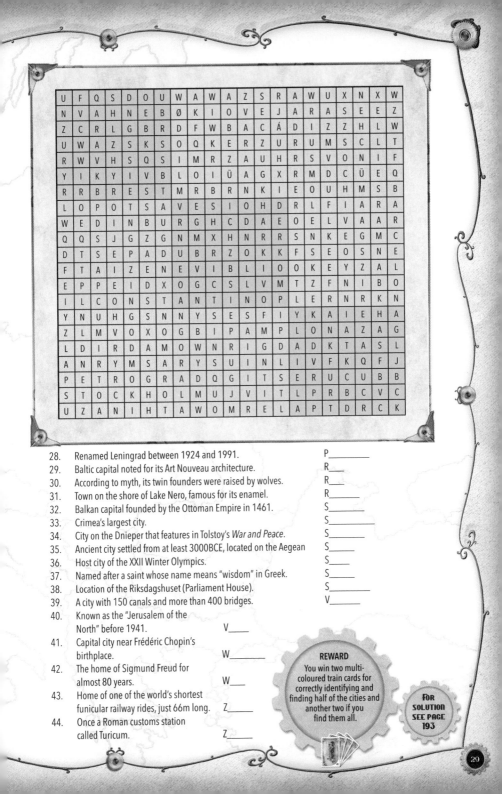

U	F	Q	S	D	O	U	W	A	W	A	Z	S	R	A	W	U	X	N	X	W
N	V	A	H	N	E	B	Ø	K	I	O	V	E	J	A	R	A	S	E	E	Z
Z	C	R	L	G	B	R	D	F	W	B	A	C	Á	D	I	Z	Z	H	L	W
U	W	A	Z	S	K	S	O	Q	K	E	R	Z	U	R	U	M	S	C	L	T
R	W	V	H	S	Q	S	I	M	R	Z	A	U	H	R	S	V	O	N	I	F
Y	I	K	Y	I	V	B	L	O	I	Ü	A	G	X	R	M	D	C	Ü	E	Q
R	R	B	R	E	S	T	M	R	B	R	N	K	I	E	O	U	H	M	S	B
L	O	P	O	T	S	A	V	E	S	I	O	H	D	R	L	F	I	A	R	A
W	E	D	I	N	B	U	R	G	H	C	D	A	E	O	E	L	V	A	A	R
Q	Q	S	J	G	Z	G	N	M	X	H	N	R	R	S	N	K	E	G	M	C
D	T	S	E	P	A	D	U	B	R	Z	O	K	K	F	S	E	O	S	N	E
F	T	A	I	Z	E	N	E	V	I	B	L	I	O	O	K	E	Y	Z	A	L
E	P	P	E	I	D	X	O	G	C	S	L	V	M	T	Z	F	N	I	B	O
I	L	C	O	N	S	T	A	N	T	I	N	O	P	L	E	R	N	R	K	N
Y	N	U	H	G	S	N	N	Y	S	E	S	F	I	Y	K	A	I	E	H	A
Z	L	M	V	O	X	O	G	B	I	P	A	M	P	L	O	N	A	Z	A	G
L	D	I	R	D	A	M	O	W	N	R	I	G	D	A	D	K	T	A	S	L
A	N	R	Y	M	S	A	R	Y	S	U	I	N	L	I	V	F	K	Q	F	J
P	E	T	R	O	G	R	A	D	Q	G	I	T	S	E	R	U	C	U	B	B
S	T	O	C	K	H	O	L	M	U	J	V	I	T	L	P	R	B	C	V	C
U	Z	A	N	I	H	T	A	W	O	M	R	E	L	A	P	T	D	R	C	K

28. Renamed Leningrad between 1924 and 1991.   P_____
29. Baltic capital noted for its Art Nouveau architecture.   R___
30. According to myth, its twin founders were raised by wolves.   R___
31. Town on the shore of Lake Nero, famous for its enamel.   R_____
32. Balkan capital founded by the Ottoman Empire in 1461.   S_____
33. Crimea's largest city.   S_____
34. City on the Dnieper that features in Tolstoy's *War and Peace*.   S_____
35. Ancient city settled from at least 3000BCE, located on the Aegean   S_____
36. Host city of the XXII Winter Olympics.   S_____
37. Named after a saint whose name means "wisdom" in Greek.   S_____
38. Location of the Riksdagshuset (Parliament House).   S_____
39. A city with 150 canals and more than 400 bridges.   V_____
40. Known as the "Jerusalem of the North" before 1941.   V_____
41. Capital city near Frédéric Chopin's birthplace.   W_____
42. The home of Sigmund Freud for almost 80 years.   W___
43. Home of one of the world's shortest funicular railway rides, just 66m long.   Z_____
44. Once a Roman customs station called Turicum.   Z_____

REWARD

You win two multi-coloured train cards for correctly identifying and finding half of the cities and another two if you find them all.

FOR SOLUTION SEE PAGE 193

MAKE TRACKS

Before you left the shores of the United States, your friends had presented you with a small present to keep you company on your travels: a puzzle book themed all around your love of trains. You were touched, but you were determined not to spend too much time with your head in the book – there was too much to see, and too many people to talk to. You were absolutely determined not to miss a thing!

However, you are currently stalled on an unmoving train at the bottom of a valley somewhere in Gloucestershire – Adlestrop was the last stop, and the only other passenger had alighted there. After 15 minutes spent completely alone, staring out at the admittedly lovely rural scenery, you decide it is time crack the book open, and turn to the first page…

Can you design a railway that connects all of the stations and rail yards?
Draw a single continuous line around the grid that passes through every station and rail yard.

If the line enters a station, turn left or right within its square before passing straight through the next square you come to. Ensure that this works for both routes going in and out of the station.

If the line enters a rail yard, keep going straight through its square before turning left or right in the next square. Ensure that this works for at least one route going into the rail yard.

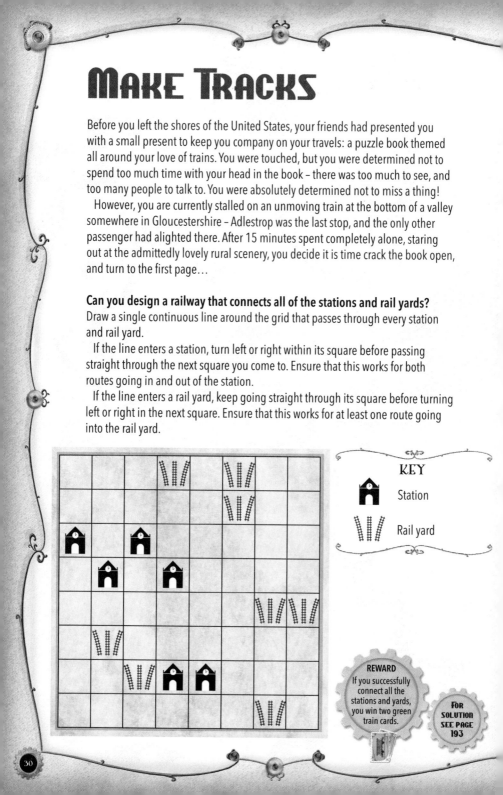

KEY

🏠 Station

⫽⫽⫽ Rail yard

REWARD
If you successfully connect all the stations and yards, you win two green train cards.

FOR SOLUTION SEE PAGE 193

HASTIER REVERY

You have made it across the Channel and you are finally on the European continent. The USA is a melting pot of cultures and languages, so you thought you were prepared for being somewhere so unfamiliar. However, while the unfamiliarity is exhilarating, you've swiftly found that it also makes it easy to get… well… lost. Which is how you've found yourself shaking a drawing of the Eiffel Tower at bemused Parisians, trying to figure out how to get there.

Help can come in the most unexpected of places, though, which is a lesson you are determined to remember in your future travels. A young, somewhat mischievous-looking girl is leading you in what you hope is the right direction. On the way she keeps turning to you and saying words that don't sound French, but don't make much sense in English either. Can you determine what she is saying?

The following list of anagrams are things you can only find in Europe. They all have something in common and there is a clue in the title, which is also an anagram.

Can you unscramble the anagrams and discover what binds them together?

1.	BAN DUE
2.	IN HER
3.	HERON
4.	SOLE ELM
5.	OILER
6.	RIPE END
7.	HAS MET
8.	BITER
9.	SEE IN
10.	GOOD NERD

REWARD
If you unscramble all the words, you win two blue train cards.

FOR SOLUTION SEE PAGE 194

THE ORIENT EXPRESS

You are travelling across continental Europe on the most prestigious train of its age: the Orient Express. As enchanting as the train is, your fellow passengers are even more impressive. Over the journey you meet an artist and a journalist, and even discover that there's a spy on board! That's certainly something new. From a few scraps of information, a story starts to unfold.

Can you place each passenger on the train, with their name, profession and journey details?

Here is what you have discovered:
1. Romanova travelled 1,000 km further than the journalist called Schmidt.
2. The fireman travelled in the carriage next to the driver and got off at Calais.
3. The driver, in his cab at the front of the train, was next to Dupont's carriage.
4. The artist travelled 215 km in Third Class discomfort at the back of the train.
5. Ozturk's ticket was for Vienna. He was not the one who travelled from Strasburg.
6. The passenger who alighted at Calais had travelled 620 km from a German town.
7. The one who travelled from Bucharest to Munich was in the next carriage to the passenger who only travelled 215 km.
8. Macduff travelled all the way from Istanbul to London.
9. The passenger travelling from Varna to Paris enjoyed First Class luxury accommodation.
10. The driver remained on the train for the entire 3,100 km journey.
11. The First-Class carriage had only one occupant by the name of Romanova. She was two carriages away from the passenger who got on at Budapest.
12. The spy travelled 2,500 km, positioned in the carriage next to the passenger who got aboard in Bucharest.
13. Schmidt and Macduff were not in adjoining carriages.

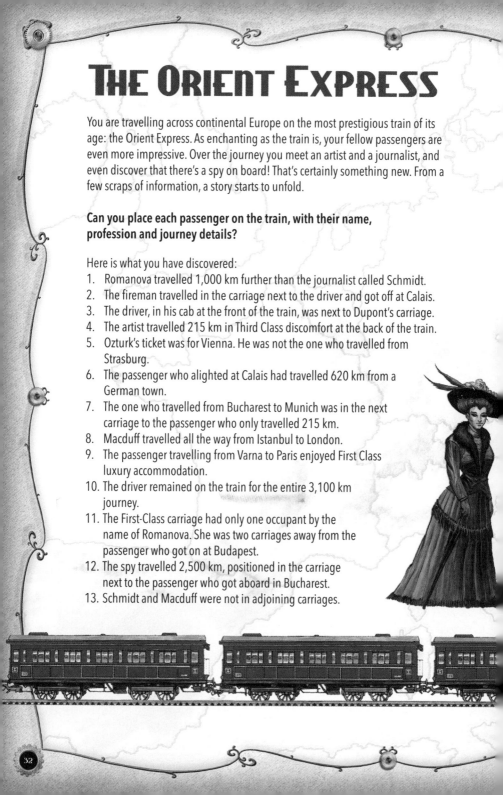

CARRIAGE	CAB	TENDER	1st CLASS	2nd CLASS	3rd CLASS
PASSENGER					
PROFESSION					
FROM					
TO					
DISTANCE					

REWARD
Find out who did what and went where to win two purple train cards.

FOR SOLUTION SEE PAGE 194

Ottoman Empire

On your journey across Europe on the Orient Express you fall in with a fellow explorer far more experienced than you in the ways of European travel, languages, culture… pretty much everything, if you are honest. Your final stop is Constantinople and as soon as you step out of the station, you are incredibly glad that she is there to guide you. The noises, colours and general commotion are like nothing you have experienced before – even among the bustling streets of New York, teeming with brash energy.

She leads you, bewildered, to the Grand Bazaar. Greeted by a labyrinthine series of alleyways, you can find everything from spices to leather goods to rows and rows of jewellery that wouldn't look out of place in Manhattan's diamond district. It is all somewhat overwhelming for you on your first day in the city, and while she is bartering in a language you don't even recognise for what looks like a pound of green tea, you decide to plan your next route, which you will be setting off on in a few days.

For the next stage of your journey, you must work out the route and insert the tracks into the grid below.

The numbers on the periphery tell you how many rail sections must be in that row or column.

You may place only a straight or a curved section inside a box.
The tracks cannot cross themselves.

Straight

Curve

Can you connect Constantinople to Ankara?

A street view taken from your time in Constantinople.

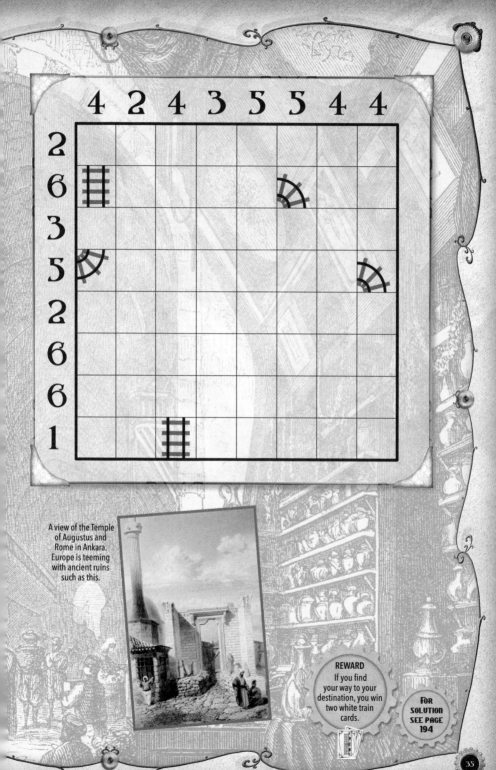

A view of the Temple of Augustus and Rome in Ankara. Europe is teeming with ancient ruins such as this.

REWARD
If you find your way to your destination, you win two white train cards.

FOR SOLUTION SEE PAGE 194

Time Warp

On a cold, clear day in the mountains, you find yourself at a deserted rail terminus somewhere in northern Europe. It is a far cry from Constantinople, which you fell in love with before you left. But, breathing in deeply, you think that there is nothing quite like the crisp air at these altitudes. Shivering, you also wonder how soon you will get out of it and back into the warmth…

The noticeboard informs you that a train will arrive every two hours. Checking your pocket watch, you find that the hour hand has broken off, rendering it all but useless. Then it starts to snow.

Fortunately, there is an extremely unusual clock on the platform, the like of which you have never seen before, showing four o'clock. You sit on the bench beneath it, glad of the meagre shelter.

After an hour, you get up to check the odd clock and are dismayed to find that it now says *three* o'clock. Your spirits, not to mention your body, are getting damper by the second, but you resolve to wait a while longer, wondering if you don't understand this clock's strange technology.

Your patience is rewarded – finally – 59 minutes later, when a train pulls into the station. After finding your seat, you ask a fellow passenger the time.

"It's almost eight o'clock," she replies.

What was wrong with the station's clock?

REWARD
If you figure it out within an hour, you win one yellow train card.

FOR SOLUTION SEE PAGE 195

CARRIAGE RETURN

In Switzerland you are taking a break from your alpine exploration, after a thrilling ride *under* and *through* a mountain via the Gotthard Tunnel. You were exhilarated by the experience, but on the whole you've decided it's far preferable to be on top of the mountain than have the mountain on top of you.

As you stretch your ever-so-slightly shaking legs, you happen to meet a rail yard supervisor with a problem. The six carriages below have been set up in the wrong order: the green carriages should have been attached to the right-hand locomotive and the yellow carriages to the one on the left.

All the carriages are now uncoupled and there is a single space large enough for a carriage to be moved into. However, what complicates things are that there are only two ways a carriage can be moved:

• You can *push* one into a space.
• You can *lift* a carriage with a crane and place it in a space.

The carriages must be moved one at a time and can only be lifted over one other carriage at a time, and the locomotives must stay where they are. You agree to help out as best you can.

What is the fewest number of moves it will take to put the carriages into the correct positions of 4-5-6 (in that order) attached to the left-hand locomotive, and 1-2-3 (in that order) attached to the right-hand locomotive?

1   2   3

DID YOU KNOW?

As well as boasting the longest rail tunnel (the Gotthard Tunnel is now 35.4 miles long), Switzerland also has the steepest cogwheel railway. The Mount Pilatus Railway has a dizzying maximum gradient of 48%, and would look at home in a theme park.

Construction of the Gotthard Tunnel beneath the Alps. You are pleased not to have been involved.

4   5   6

REWARD
If you solve it for the supervisor in the least number of moves, you win one black train card.

FOR SOLUTION SEE PAGE 195

Tongue-tied

Europe is home to a remarkable diversity of languages, and you've met a globe-trotter who claims to be able to speak all of them. You don't quite believe him, but you have already seen many remarkable things on your travels, and he is very convincing. He even teaches you about their origins.

Most belong to the broad family of languages known as "Indo-European" and have been shaped by Latin due to the influence of the Roman Empire. Notable exceptions are the Uralic languages, such as Hungarian, Finnish and Estonian, whose precise origins have long been a puzzle to linguists.

Can you arrange the words below into three groups of five and five groups of three?

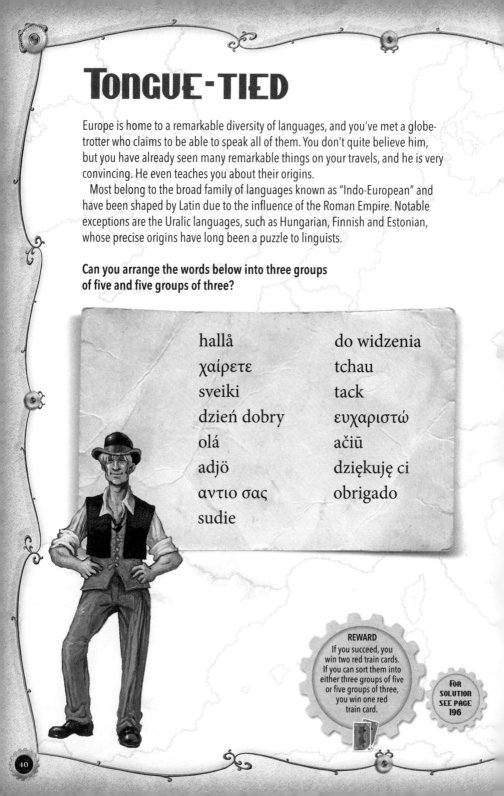

hallå	do widzenia
χαίρετε	tchau
sveiki	tack
dzień dobry	ευχαριστώ
olá	ačiū
adjö	dziękuję ci
αντιο σας	obrigado
sudie	

REWARD
If you succeed, you win two red train cards. If you can sort them into either three groups of five or five groups of three, you win one red train card.

FOR SOLUTION SEE PAGE 196

MYTHOMANIA

The next station on your journey is Zürich, where you will need to take the 11 o'clock train to Berlin. You arrive at the station, clutching your ticket, with just minutes to spare.

Two trains are waiting on different platforms with no indication of their destination. You approach a smartly-dressed man who you believe must have the answers you need. Indeed his demeanour implies he has the answers to everything in life! He looks you up and down and replies:

"No idea."

However, he does tell you:

"There's a uniformed attendant on both platforms, but I should warn you that one of them has an affliction that makes him a compulsive liar – he literally cannot give a truthful answer! The other attendant is scrupulously honest though."

When you ask which attendant has the unfortunate affliction, he winks:

"No idea."

You only have enough time to ask one of the attendants a question and cross the bridge to the other platform if required.

How do you ensure that you get onto the correct train?

REWARD
If you figure it out in three minutes, you win two multi-coloured train cards. If it takes you longer, you win one multi-coloured train card.

FOR SOLUTION SEE PAGE 196

JIGSAW JUMBLE

You have experienced a whirlwind tour of Europe, and it has only whetted your appetite for more. How can you be expected to take in an entire continent in mere weeks? Especially when you are spending so much time trying to understand mysterious clocks or unscramble foreign languages, so as not to miss your next train. You decide that your next trip will take place in just one country.

   You were particularly taken by the sights, smells and sounds of Constantinople, which was your first foray into the Islamic world. Its rich history is reflected in its magnificent architecture, with no better example than the Blue Mosque, so large that it can hold 10,000 worshippers at once.

Nine of the jigsaw pieces on the right fit into the picture of the mosque below, but three of them do not.

Which are the odd ones out?

A

DID YOU KNOW?

The Orient Express originally terminated in Constantinople (now Istanbul) and was the most luxurious mode of travel across Europe for much of the 20th century. If you book it now, though, be warned: there are still no WiFi or showers available!

B

C

D

E

F

G

H

I

J

K

L

REWARD
If you find the odd pieces, you win two orange train cards.

FOR SOLUTION SEE PAGE 196

GERMANY

The region now known as Germany has played a significant role in the story of Europe. Way back in the first century CE, *Germania* did its best to resist the might of Imperial Rome, yet by the tenth century it had become the seat of the Holy Roman Empire. This paradigm of Catholic imperialism was the instigator of many of Europe's most influential ideas, notably the sixteenth century's Protestant Reformation and then as an integral contributor to the creation of socialism three centuries later.

Galvanized by the Industrial Revolution, the states of Germany unified at the end of the nineteenth century, and it entered the twentieth century as a Great Power. With such a varied and tumultuous history, there is much to see and do in Germany, and you are keen to make it the first stop in your detailed European exploration!

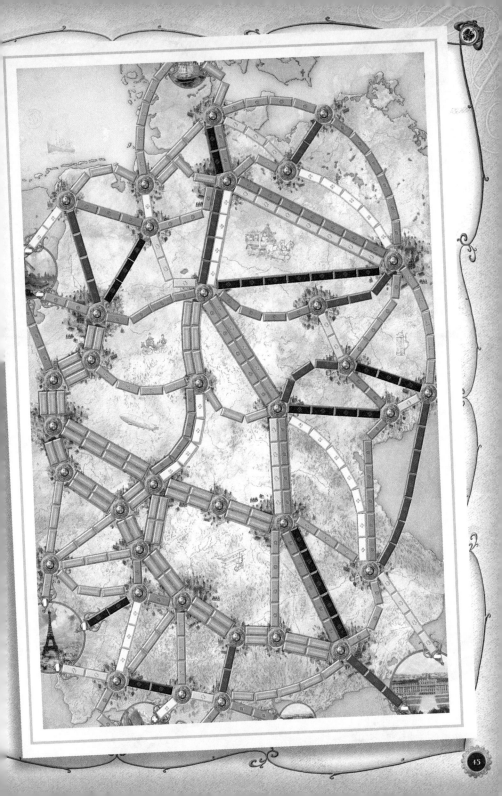

DISCOVER GERMANY

The imperial capital Berlin is a metropolis *par excellence* (your language lessons have improved, although… you worry you may have taken a wrong turn somewhere), but there is one disappointment for you. The subway – or *U-Bahn*, as it is beginning to be known – is only due to open the following year. You had been looking forward to the chance to ride the underground train. Then again, given your experience in the subterranean mountain tunnels, perhaps it's for the best.

You take a seat in the shadows of the Brandenburg Gate and open up a guidebook to begin to make your plans. You pretend to yourself that you are pleased that the map is in German.

The Brandenburg Gate in Berlin, a symbol of unity and peace, and your backdrop while planning your route.

The names of 34 cities (in German) are concealed in the grid opposite. They may run horizontally, vertically, diagonally, forwards or backwards. To make things more challenging, you must work out which cities are included by matching them with their facts below.

1.	An eponymous peace treaty was signed here in 1555.	A_____
2.	A city divided in two between 1961 and 1989.	B_____
3.	In a Grimms' fairy tale, four animals wanted to become musicians here.	B_____
4.	Founded by Johann Smidt in 1827.	B_____
5.	Renamed Karl-Marx-Stadt between 1953 and 1990.	C_____
6.	Home of the German Football Museum.	D_____
7.	Capital city of Saxony, famous for its Baroque architecture.	D_____
8.	Famous for children doing cartwheels since the thirteenth century.	D_____
9.	East Frisia's main city and seaport.	E____
10.	Capital of Thuringia, where Martin Luther studied.	E_____
11.	The city internationally associated with hot-dog style sausages.	F_____
12.	The Albert Ludwig University was founded here in 1457.	F_____
13.	Home of the world's largest model railway, *Miniatur Wunderland*.	H_____
14.	Home to the world's largest exhibition ground.	H_____
15.	Location of the Federal Constitutional Court.	K_____
16.	The *Bergpark Wilhelmshöhe* hillside park can be found here.	K_____
17.	Host of the world's biggest annual sailing event.	K___
18.	Name originates from the confluence of the Rhine and Moselle.	K_____
19.	The home of *Kölsch* beer.	K___
20.	City on Lake Constance where the Papal Schism was ended.	K_____
21.	Location of Europe's largest (in surface area) train station.	L_____
22.	Island town named after a tree of the genus *Tilia*.	L____
23.	Final resting place of Holy Roman Emperor Otto I, (Otto the Great).	M_____

T	J	H	B	B	A	N	E	K	C	Ü	R	B	R	A	A	S	L	M	G	S
O	W	N	I	L	R	E	B	R	W	U	R	S	L	E	S	S	A	K	R	Z
D	Ü	S	S	E	L	D	O	R	F	I	M	M	C	W	J	J	G	J	L	U	E
Z	W	B	C	T	U	Q	S	H	R	W	F	D	F	H	D	Z	I	Z	B	H
L	M	N	E	V	A	H	R	E	M	E	R	B	A	E	W	A	N	V	Z	U
I	H	M	Z	B	D	K	T	K	F	G	Q	H	B	U	L	E	Ü	V	R	R
N	M	E	X	D	K	S	A	H	Z	S	T	U	T	T	G	A	R	T	Ü	S
D	F	S	K	Y	N	N	X	M	D	T	R	W	H	V	V	S	N	I	W	L
A	R	L	J	Ü	S	B	F	Y	D	G	I	Z	O	E	E	K	B	D	N	R
U	A	T	M	K	R	Y	N	Y	G	O	X	N	V	S	W	G	E	U	G	A
G	N	H	R	L	B	A	B	C	G	F	R	A	M	Z	J	C	R	G	R	G
R	K	E	Q	U	L	H	C	A	R	J	D	T	G	E	Z	A	G	S	W	G
U	F	D	M	T	F	Y	I	I	U	W	D	S	M	R	H	N	X	B	T	H
B	U	Y	O	E	E	R	O	U	B	M	Q	N	R	U	U	C	I	F	W	N
S	R	L	Ñ	Z	R	K	E	L	M	W	K	O	E	D	N	B	U	A	L	R
N	T	O	E	F	L	B	K	M	A	A	N	K	V	V	R	D	I	Ö	M	G
E	P	X	F	I	G	V	I	F	H	T	L	Y	O	V	I	E	K	E	M	G
G	M	X	I	R	P	K	S	M	I	E	H	N	N	A	M	U	S	G	R	M
E	O	D	F	M	K	Z	I	K	O	B	L	E	N	Z	Z	G	Q	D	G	F
R	Z	G	E	D	O	G	I	E	P	B	H	U	A	Y	A	R	L	N	E	E
N	E	H	C	N	Ü	M	A	G	L	U	R	R	H	Z	S	P	E	N	Y	N

24. Birthplace of the Gutenberg Bible in the 1450s. M____
25. Nicknamed "the Square City" because of its grid-like street layout. M_____
26. Southern city that plays host to the annual Oktoberfest celebrations. M_____
27. Germany's "cycling capital" in North Rhine-Westphalia. M_____
28. Location of DB Museum, Germany's oldest railway museum. N_____
29. Site of a famous twelfth-century stone bridge. R_____
30. Capital city of the Saarland. S_____
31. Oldest city and capital of Mecklenburg-Vorpommern. S_____
32. Birthplace and headquarters of Porsche AG. S_____
33. Location of the world's highest church steeple. U__
34. Administrative seat of Lower Franconia. W_____

REWARD
You win two blue train cards for correctly identifying and finding half of the cities and another two if you find them all.

FOR SOLUTION SEE PAGE 197

MAKE TRACKS

It is your first German domestic trip – on the *Lehrter Bahn* to Hanover – and you are very pleased with yourself, having held a passable conversation in German with an older woman at the train station before you left. Well, you asked her where the water closet was and understood her pointed finger giving you the direction you needed. But in your eyes: progress! Rather than bury yourself once more in your German dictionary, you decide to celebrate with one of your friends' puzzles.

Can you design a railway that connects all of the stations and rail yards?
Draw a single continuous line around the grid that passes through every station and rail yard.

If the line enters a station, turn left or right within its square before passing straight through the next square you come to. Ensure that this works for both routes going in and out of the station.

If the line enters a rail yard, keep going straight through its square before turning left or right in the next square. Ensure that this works for at least one route going into the rail yard.

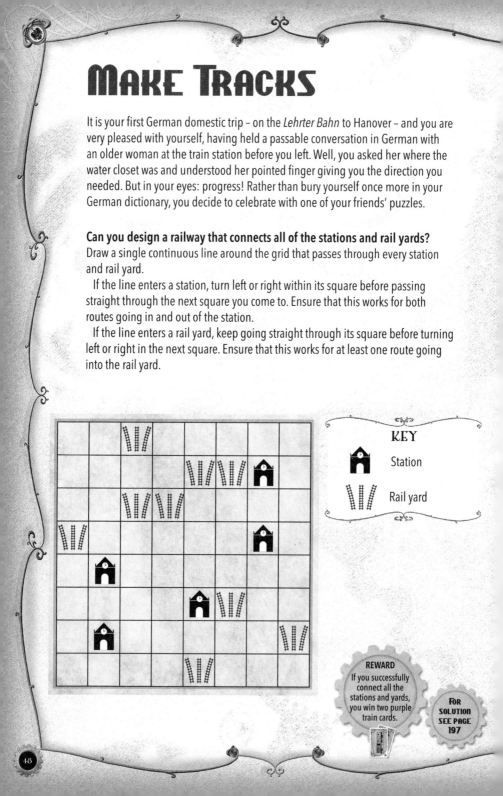

KEY

🏠 Station

〰 Rail yard

REWARD
If you successfully connect all the stations and yards, you win two purple train cards.

FOR SOLUTION SEE PAGE 197

Find Rank Dodo

Having spent the day travelling south to Frankfurt, you are exhausted and check in at your hotel before heading out briefly for a quick dinner, followed by a well-earned sleep. Alas, as seems to happen to you wherever you go, you are joined at your table by a well-dressed man. Normally, you would be delighted to have a dinner companion but, in this instance, your tiredness and his perplexing conversational skills make it extremely difficult to follow the thread of what he is saying.

The following list of anagrams are things associated with Germany. They all have something in common and there is a clue in the title, which is also an anagram.

Can you unscramble the anagrams and say what binds them together?

1.	ENTREE WINS ZILCH	
2.	UK HALFPENCE	
3.	BURST WART	
4.	MILK CREEP PUN	
5.	TAURUS RAKE	
6.	LENS RIP	
7.	HOST TRICKER	
8.	SIR NIGEL	
9.	LEZ TREP	
10.	A GRIM BUM	

REWARD
If you unscramble all the names, you win two red train cards.

FOR SOLUTION SEE PAGE 198

OKTOBERFEST

Each year the city of Munich plays host to the world's largest folk festival with more than 15 days of Bavarian culture and copious amounts of German sausages and frivolity! It is something you have decided simply cannot be missed.

   You check into a guesthouse, then spend all day enjoying the entertainment with your fellow travellers, not to mention a significant part of the night. By the end of the celebration you have made many new friends and feel so full that you can barely roll home.

   When you rise the next morning, the other guests have already checked out. As Ingrid, the landlady, serves you breakfast with a smile, she asks you about your day and you fall into a deep conversation, entertaining her with all of the day's events. Who were the other guests, where were they from, how many sausages did they eat and what ridiculous adventures did they have?

Can you fill in all the facts from the clues below?
1. Gustav's sense of direction was not particularly good, and he got lost on the way back to the guesthouse. He was not the guest from Düsseldorf, who ate only half as many as Otto.
2. The guest from Cologne wasn't sick from over-eating, even though they ate more than the one from Ulm.
3. Although she was a local, Birgit still liked to stay at the guesthouse for the festival.
4. The guest who ate six bratwurst proposed to Ingrid. She politely declined.
5. Hedwig devoured an impressive 12 frankfurters. She wasn't the Berliner who ended up on top of one of the parade floats doing the *schuhplattler*.

Guest	From	Number of sausages	Adventure
Heinz			
Birgit			
Hedwig			
Otto			
Gustav			

	Düsseldorf	Cologne	Ulm	Munich	Berlin	5 sausages	6 sausages	8 sausages	10 sausages	12 sausages	Proposed	Entered parade	Swam in canal	Was sick	Got lost
Heinz															
Birgit															
Hedwig															
Otto															
Gustav															
Proposed															
Entered parade															
Swam in canal															
Was sick															
Got lost															
5 sausages															
6 sausages															
8 sausages															
10 sausages															
12 sausages															

REWARD
If you remember all the facts, you win three multicoloured train cards.

FOR SOLUTION SEE PAGE 198

REUNIFICATION

After experiencing Oktoberfest for a couple more evenings, you decide that it would be best to move on before you become a bit too used to its delights. On a whim, you book a train to Leipzig, realising too late that you have somehow booked a circuitous route via Frankfurt.

No matter, you think, the sights through the train window never fail to please you, and you might even be able to catch up on some much needed sleep on the way. Those hopes are dashed when an irrepressible young boy with an intimate knowledge of the German rail system (who wants to tell you all of the various ways you should have travelled to Leipzig instead) joins you in your carriage.

Before long, you find yourself comparing journey times, trackside sights and refreshment trolleys with him, and while away a surprisingly happy couple of hours.

For the next stage of your journey, you must work out the route and insert the tracks into the grid below. The numbers on the periphery tell you how many rail sections must be in that row or column.

You may place only a straight or a curved section inside a box.
The tracks cannot cross themselves.

Straight

Curve

Can you connect Frankfurt to Leipzig?

Frankfurt Zoo, where you saw an elephant for the first time!

	6	4	4	4	2	4	6	4
5								
6								
8								
5								
3								
5								
1								
1								

The busy City Hall and marketplace in Leipzig, where you bought some *lederhosen*.

REWARD
If you find your way to your destination, you win two green train cards.

FOR SOLUTION SEE PAGE 198

Brocken Down

For your next excursion you take the Brocken Railway, which runs through the Harz mountain range in northern Germany and brings you all the way to the summit of its highest peak, the Brocken (or Blocksberg).

In a café with a breathtaking view of the region's snow-covered surroundings, the locals are happy to tell you about the region's folklore, including the witches and giants that have haunted the remote area since the Middle Ages. You are delighted to discover that some of their tales are actually riddles.

Over a mug of hot chocolate, a woman tells you a tall story about the ghost of a crazy engine driver who was trying to get his ramshackle steam train up the mountain to the station. The train began its journey on a Monday morning one kilometre from the terminus. Caught in a perpetual blizzard the train manages to climb a pitiful 300 metres each day, but during the night it slides 200 metres back down the track.

"The engine driver never gives up though," the woman says firmly. "He might be dead, but he's still German!"

On what day does the train reach its final destination?

REWARD
If you figure it out, you win one orange train card.

FOR SOLUTION SEE PAGE 199

Excess Baggage

Now that Oktoberfest is over, you have decided to return to Ingrid's guesthouse and actually do some sightseeing. Ingrid beams upon seeing you, and moves to bring you a sausage from her kitchen. Quickly, you stop her, not wanting to see another sausage for at least a month, and instead catch her up on all of your adventures since you left.

A few days later, you head out on an overnight trip to Stuttgart with the purpose of seeing the magnificent New Palace. Unfortunately, you must not have been the only person to have that thought: you are one of eight hundred passengers on the crowded train. Fortunately, as an experienced traveller, you have had the forethought to book a seat. However, the train guard tells you that there is only enough storage space in the overhead racks for one item of luggage per passenger. You have no issue with this, but the edict has not prevented some passengers from bringing more than the recommended amount.

Including you, 15 per cent of the passengers have a single item of luggage. Half of the remaining 85 per cent have two items of luggage, while the other passengers are travelling without luggage. The guard is at a loss to know what to do next.

How many excess items of luggage have been brought onto the train?

REWARD
If you help the guard and figure it out, you win one black train card.

FOR SOLUTION SEE PAGE 199

MYSTERIES OF THE ILLUMINATI

You have heard of the Illuminati. It is a not-so-secret society that has found its way into tall tales and has already fuelled innumerable conspiracy theories of shadowy puppet masters bent on world domination. However, from some research you have learned that the real Illuminati was founded by Bavarian philosopher Adam Weishaupt in 1776 and its goal was to promote Enlightenment ideas and oppose the power of the clergy.

Like any good secret society, the Order of the Illuminati kept its secrets hidden through the use of codes and ciphers. This thought plays on your imagination as you travel through Bavaria and are drawn to any evidence of arcane activity.

Your investigation appears to be rewarded at the rail station in Munich, where you find a sequence of glyphs etched into a stone wall. Could this be a message from the secret order?

Are you enlightened enough to draw the missing symbol?

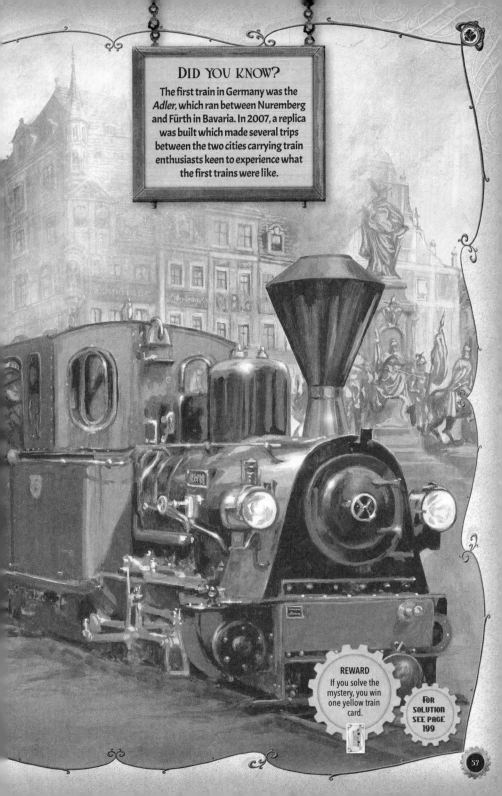

DID YOU KNOW?

The first train in Germany was the *Adler*, which ran between Nuremberg and Fürth in Bavaria. In 2007, a replica was built which made several trips between the two cities carrying train enthusiasts keen to experience what the first trains were like.

REWARD
If you solve the mystery, you win one yellow train card.

FOR SOLUTION SEE PAGE 199

LOCOMOTION

As a reward for helping the guard with the luggage issue, he has agreed to take you to a depot to explore a selection of trains when they are not in use. You get a shiver of a thrill as you board the first one, knowing that the entire train is yours to explore. There are so many trains of different shapes and sizes around that you feel like you could spend the entire day here!

Map and explore the trains in the depot. Ten trains must be placed in the grid opposite. The numbers on the periphery tell you how many squares in that row or column contain a train component (locomotive or carriage). No two trains' components can occupy neighbouring squares (including diagonals).

Can you find…

One train consisting of a locomotive and three carriages.

Two trains consisting of a locomotive with two carriages.

Three trains consisting of a locomotive with one carriage.

Four locomotives with no carriages.

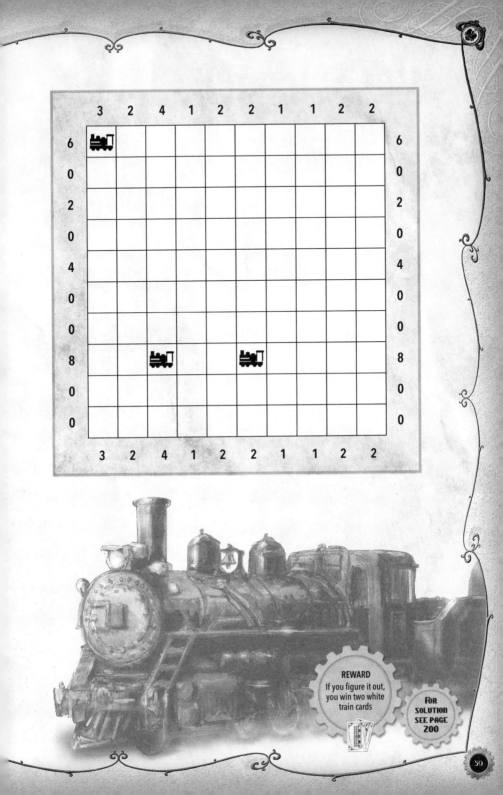

FOR
SOLUTION
SEE PAGE
200

REWARD
If you figure it out,
you win two white
train cards

ALL CHANGE!

Your German wanderlust is at an end, for the time being at least. Your final stop is Münster, where you are resting for a few days before embarking on the next leg of your grand adventure. You are sad to be leaving, because you feel you have finally mastered the German language, but you think you have now travelled almost every inch of its fantastically regulated rail system.

One particular highlight was the secluded Neuschwanstein Castle, which was only recently opened to the public. Walking its halls had made you feel like royalty, and so you bought some paintings of it as keepsakes.

Apart from the slightly different perspectives around the paintings' borders, how quickly can you find 12 differences between the picture on the left and the one on the right?

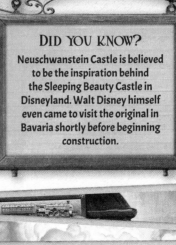

DID YOU KNOW?

Neuschwanstein Castle is believed to be the inspiration behind the Sleeping Beauty Castle in Disneyland. Walt Disney himself even came to visit the original in Bavaria shortly before beginning construction.

REWARD

If you find all 12 differences in fewer than 10 minutes, you win four orange train cards. If you succeed in more than 10 minutes, you win two orange train cards.

FOR SOLUTION SEE PAGE 200

FRANCE

Julius Caesar conquered *Gallia* (Gaul), a region in Western Europe, by 50 BCE. When the Roman Empire fell into decline, the incoming Frankish tribes gave this region the name Francia, which would eventually morph into its modern name.

After centuries of feudalism and hereditary monarchy, a revolution occurred in 1789 that would later define the country's character. Over the next century, the nation would undergo many transformations, including becoming an empire under Napoleon, as well as a temporary return to monarchy. But France would never stop striving to perfect its revolutionary ideals of "*Liberté, égalité, fraternité*", aspirations that inspired the US Constitution and provided a framework for nascent democracies all around the world.

France is also a land of breathtaking natural landscapes as well as magnificent art and architecture from its various *époques*.

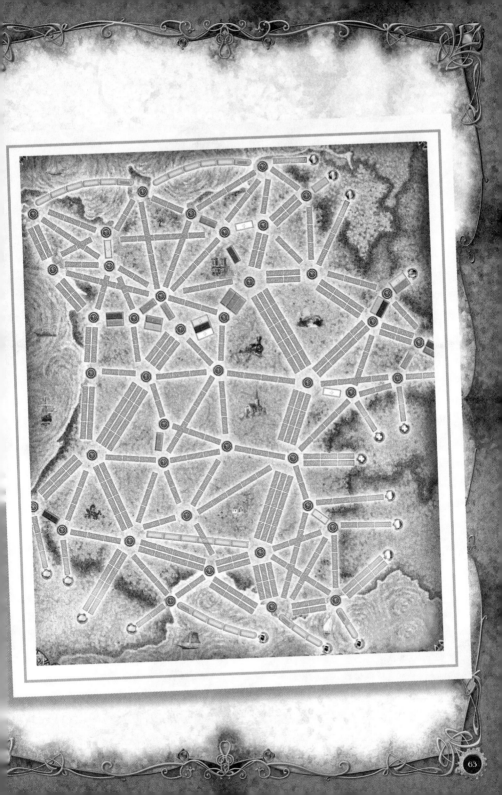

DISCOVER FRANCE

You begin your French tour in Strasbourg, a city famed for its cathedral and its well-maintained medieval architecture, particularly in the Petite France district. It is there – after a pleasurable boat trip around the area that afforded you a brief glimpse of the sights – that you plan your journey around the country.

The names of 42 cities (in French) are concealed in the grid opposite. They may run horizontally, vertically, diagonally, forward or backwards. To make things more challenging, you must work out which cities are included by matching them with their facts below.

1.	Location of the largest cathedral in France.	A_____
2.	Home of the medieval Apocalypse Tapestry.	A_____
3.	A famous folk song celebrates dancing on a bridge here.	A_____
4.	In August, people dress in white and red for the summer festival here.	B_____
5.	French capital of watchmaking, home to the complex watch Leroy 01.	B_____
6.	Famous wine-producing port city in the Gironde.	B_____
7.	Capital of the historic province of Berry until 1790.	B_____
8.	Situated at the top of a peninsula, home of the *Océanopolis* aquarium.	B____
9.	The highest city in France (1,326 metres).	B_____
10.	Host of a book fair where the Prix de la langue française is awarded.	B____ __ _____
11.	The White Cliffs of Dover can be seen from this port.	C_____
12.	A port city; in the title of a famous 1960s film linked to umbrellas.	C_____
13.	City in the Auvergne surrounded by volcanoes.	C_____ _____
14.	City in the Côte-d'Or famous for its mustard.	D____
15.	Known locally as the "Capital of the Alps".	G_____
16.	Twelfth-century Atlantic naval base of the Knights Templar.	L_ _____
17.	"The harbour"; founded by King Francis I on the estuary of the Seine.	L_ _____
18.	Host of the world's oldest still-active endurance sports car race.	L_ ____
19.	The birthplace of Charles de Gaulle, also known in France as the "Capital of Flanders".	L____
20.	Originally settled by the Romans, its porcelain made it world famous.	L_____
21.	Host of the Festival Interceltique since the early 1970s.	L_____
22.	City that was the capital of Roman Gaul, known for its gastronomy.	L___
23.	Southern coastal city with the most sunshine in France.	M_____
24.	City located near the border junction of France, Germany and Luxembourg.	M___
25.	Home to the oldest still-active medical school in the world.	M_____
26.	Home of the *Cité du Train* railway museum.	M_____
27.	Location of the beautiful *Place Stanislas*.	N____
28.	A major seaport on the Loire estuary.	N_____
29.	Traditional winter residence for English aristocracy, has a promenade named the "Walkway of the English".	N___
30.	Joan of Arc helped to lift the siege of this city.	O_____
31.	City named Lutetia by the Romans.	P____

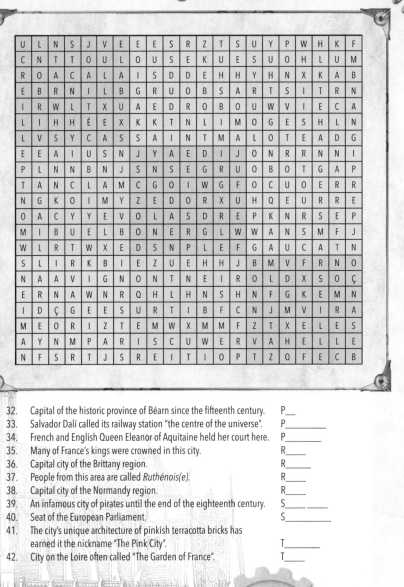

U	L	N	S	J	V	E	E	E	S	R	Z	T	S	U	Y	P	W	H	K	F
C	N	T	T	O	U	L	O	U	S	E	K	U	E	S	U	O	H	L	U	M
R	O	A	C	A	L	A	I	S	D	D	E	H	H	Y	H	N	X	K	A	B
E	B	R	N	I	L	B	G	R	U	O	B	S	A	R	T	S	I	T	R	N
I	R	W	L	T	X	U	A	E	D	R	O	B	O	U	W	V	I	E	C	A
L	I	H	H	É	E	X	K	K	T	N	L	I	M	O	G	E	S	H	L	N
L	V	S	Y	C	A	S	S	A	I	N	T	M	A	L	O	T	E	A	D	G
E	E	A	I	U	S	N	J	J	Y	A	E	D	I	J	O	N	R	R	N	I
P	L	N	N	B	N	J	S	N	S	E	G	R	U	O	B	O	T	G	A	P
T	A	N	C	L	A	M	C	G	O	I	W	G	F	O	C	U	O	E	R	R
N	G	K	O	I	M	Y	Z	E	D	O	R	X	U	H	Q	E	U	R	R	E
O	A	C	Y	Y	E	V	O	L	A	S	D	R	E	P	K	N	R	S	E	P
M	I	B	U	E	L	B	O	N	E	R	G	L	W	W	A	N	S	M	F	J
W	L	R	T	W	X	E	D	S	N	P	L	E	F	G	A	U	C	A	T	N
S	L	I	R	K	B	I	E	Z	U	E	H	H	J	B	M	V	F	R	N	O
N	A	A	V	I	G	N	O	N	T	N	E	I	R	O	L	D	X	S	O	Ç
E	R	N	A	W	N	R	Q	H	L	H	N	S	H	N	F	G	K	E	M	N
I	D	Ç	G	E	E	S	U	R	T	I	B	F	C	N	J	M	V	I	R	A
M	E	O	R	I	Z	T	E	M	W	X	M	M	F	Z	T	X	E	L	E	S
A	Y	N	M	P	A	R	I	S	C	U	W	E	R	V	A	H	E	L	L	E
N	F	S	R	T	J	S	R	E	I	T	I	O	P	T	Z	Q	F	E	C	B

32. Capital of the historic province of Béarn since the fifteenth century. P__
33. Salvador Dalí called its railway station "the centre of the universe". P_____
34. French and English Queen Eleanor of Aquitaine held her court here. P_____
35. Many of France's kings were crowned in this city. R____
36. Capital city of the Brittany region. R_____
37. People from this area are called *Ruthénois(e)*. R____
38. Capital city of the Normandy region. R____
39. An infamous city of pirates until the end of the eighteenth century. S____ ____
40. Seat of the European Parliament. S_____
41. The city's unique architecture of pinkish terracotta bricks has earned it the nickname "The Pink City". T_____
42. City on the Loire often called "The Garden of France". T____

REWARD
You win two black train cards for identifying and finding half of the towns and cities and another two if you can find them all.

FOR SOLUTION SEE PAGE 201

65

MAKE TRACKS

Lyon is an industrious and ancient city – not many places can boast that not one, but two Roman emperors were born there. For you, though, its main attractions are the funicular railways that criss-cross the city, complete with trains that suddenly appear from the first floor of buildings and travel directly over the heads of the pedestrians on the street below. The five funicular lines are confusing, though, and you soon end up happily lost as they ferry you around the city.

Can you map your journey along a railway that connects all of the funicular junctions and stations?
Draw a single continuous line around the grid that passes through every junction and station.

   If the line enters a station, turn left or right within its square before passing straight through the next square you come to. Ensure that this works for both routes going in and out of the station.

   If the line enters a junction, keep going straight through its square before turning left or right in the next square. Ensure that this works for at least one route going into the junction.

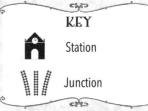

KEY

Station

Junction

FOR SOLUTION SEE PAGE 201

NASTY GROOM

La Ville Rose of Toulouse holds many attractions for you – or at least, it will, when you eventually get there. You had stopped for an early lunch of bread, cheese and strong French coffee in Rodez before catching the afternoon train on to Toulouse. However, when you are deep in the sleepily attractive countryside, you feel the train chugging to a halt. Sticking your head out of the window, you see two railway workers performing some complex engineering works and you watch in fascination.

After a quarter of an hour, the fascination has somewhat diminished, and you test out your French to ask them how much longer they will be. They wink at each other before giving a seemingly incomprehensible series of replies.

The following list of anagrams are things connected to France. They all have something in common and there is a clue in the title, which is also an anagram. Be warned – accents have been removed!

Can you unscramble the anagrams and reveal what binds them together?

1.	OUR BING FUGUE BOON	
2.	TUBE GATE	
3.	ACTORS SIN	
4.	EEL CEREBRUM	
5.	CAR MOANS	
6.	A NAUTICAL POOCH	
7.	FLU FOES	
8.	A FOG RISE	
9.	CAT MEMBER	
10.	GIRAFFES ROAM	

REWARD
If you unscramble all of the anagrams, you win two green train cards.

FOR SOLUTION SEE PAGE 202

TOUR DE FRANCE

You have grown curious about the bicycles that are ubiquitous everywhere you go in France. You have even considered spending the entire summer on a bicycle holiday, peddling along the 2,400-kilometre proposed route of a new race that you have heard being discussed in cafés around the country: the Tour de France.

And so, when you come across a family of cyclists while walking the Canal du Midi one day, you borrow the bicycle of the daughter of the family to try it out for the first time. It's only after they have to fish both you and the bike out of the water that you decide it's perhaps best to leave the cycling to the French. Instead you decide to follow the proposed route by rail, sampling the local cuisine as you go.

At the end of the trip, you reflect on your gastronomic adventure and decide to update your neglected journal before the memories fade into a haze of flavours. To make things more interesting, we will test your knowledge of French food.

Can you fill in all the facts from the memories below?
1. In Nantes you enjoyed a vegetarian stew. That was later in the year than when you tried the baked dessert made from beaten egg whites and flavoured yolks.
2. You stayed in Paris for most of the month of March
3. In Lyon, you recall eating an apple-based dessert named after the sisters who invented it, but you didn't have beef stew or a toasted ham and cheese sandwich while you were there.
4. You tentatively sampled a dish made from snails some time before you visited the last city of your tour; it was in the same restaurant where you had a meringue-based confection for dessert.
5. You know you weren't in Marseille during the month of February, but you do remember having a delicious cake with a molten middle that month.
6. In May you had a casserole of chicken in red wine.
7. You didn't have the beef stew in Paris or Bordeaux.

Location	Dinner	Dessert	Month
Paris			
Lyon			
Marseille			
Bordeaux			
Nantes			

	Croque monsieur	Escargot	Ratatouille	Coq au vin	Boeuf bourguignon	Profiteroles	Fondant au chocolat	Tarte tatin	Macarons	Soufflé	February	March	April	May	June
Paris															
Lyon															
Marseille															
Bordeaux															
Nantes															
February															
March															
April															
May															
June															
Profiteroles															
Fondant au chocolat															
Tarte tatin															
Macarons															
Soufflé															

REWARD
If you match all the meals, you win three red train cards.

FOR SOLUTION SEE PAGE 202

BRITTANY

The ancient region of Brittany is a predominantly agricultural area that relied on rural roads and canals for transportation until the first rail line connected it to Paris in 1863. After that, the map of local train routes multiplied rapidly, and you have spent a number of weeks hopping from town to village, familiarising yourself with each of them.

You decide to end your journey at Rennes, partly to see the magnificent opera house – the smallest in France, but one that packs a punch nevertheless – and partly to glimpse the "wobbly" half-timbered houses of the Place du Champ Jacquet. However, when you arrive at the local station you come across a problem: the line is under repair.

Can you work out a local rail route to get there by inserting tracks into the grid opposite? The numbers on the periphery tell you how many rail sections must be in that row or column.

You may place only a straight or a curved section inside a box.
The tracks cannot cross themselves.

Straight

Curve

Can you connect Brest to Rennes?

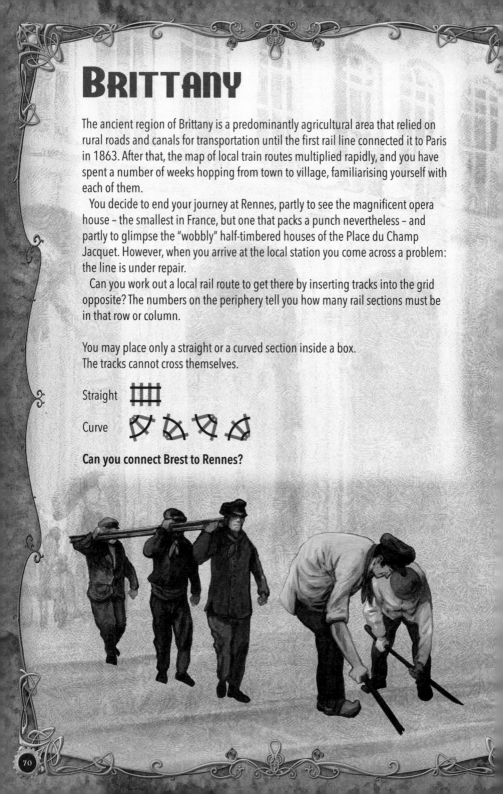

The Place des Portes
in Brest.

	2	6	2	3	5	7	4	2
1								
7								
2								
4								
6								
5								
3								
3								

The crooked houses at the
Place du Champ Jacquet
could do with a visit from an
architect.

REWARD
If you connect
the two cities, you
win two purple
train cards.

FOR
SOLUTION
SEE PAGE
202

PARIS MATCH

The "Chemin de fer" brings you at last to France's capital, a bubbling casserole of art, industry, culture and romance. Each of the city's quarters and arrondissements has a unique character while remaining distinctly Parisian. After taking in the magnificent architecture, and stopping at a café to fortify yourself, you visit a gallery in the 8th arrondissement where you discover an intriguing modern artwork.

One of the local women spots your interest: "That's one of our most avant-garde young artists. She is making quite a name for herself, although it is not to everyone's tastes." She looks at you with an appraising eye. "But I can see that you appreciate it. This piece is both a tribute to the city's diversity – and a puzzle."

Can you fill the grid below so that the letters P, A, R, I and S occur only once in each line, each column and each coloured region?

REWARD
If you complete the grid, you win one multi-coloured train card.

FOR SOLUTION SEE PAGE 203

EIFFEL TOWER

No visit to Paris would be complete without visiting the 7th arrondissement and its famous towering landmark. Completed a dozen years ago in time for the 1889 World's Fair, the Eiffel Tower is the tallest structure in the world. It dwarfs even the skyscrapers of New York, rising almost three times higher than the Park Row Building, which is currently the tallest building in the world.

From the top, you are rewarded with a panoramic view of the capital. One of your fellow travellers has brought a picnic all the way to the top – quite the impressive feat! – and is now engrossed in a guidebook with facts about the structure. You decide to strike up a conversation, only partially in the hopes of getting a bite to eat.

"Do you know how tall it is?" you ask.

"Ah, you're the famous puzzle solver!" she remarks. "Well, it's 162 meters tall, plus half its own height."

How tall is that?

A postcard you picked up showing the Eiffel Tower from Point Passay during the Paris Exposition in 1900.

REWARD
If you figure it out – or if you already know the answer – you win one orange train card.

FOR SOLUTION SEE PAGE 203

BORDEAUX

Heading south-west brings you to the historic region of Aquitaine, whose largest city, Bordeaux, is internationally renowned for its winemaking. You visit one of the region's famous vineyards, where you find a storehouse full of beautifully crafted wooden casks, with the rich scent of oakwood and fermenting grapes hanging on the air.

You are given a horse on which to ride the extensive grounds, and have a merry time being shown the complex processes that are used to create the world-famous drink. At the end of the day, hot and exhausted, you return to the main house, looking forward to a bite of supper and a good sleep. Before you can relax, though, you want to take care of the horse that has carried you all day. You lead it to a nearby water barrel and are surprised when it just stares doubtfully at it.

"Ah, that's Demi. She is our best horse, and she knows her worth. She will never drink out of a water barrel that is less than half full!" your guide tells you.

You look into the container and it appears to be more or less half-full. "Are you serious?" you ask. "How can I prove it to her?"

"There's one easy way." replies the guide.

Can you quickly determine whether the barrel is more or less than half-full, without using any measuring tools?

DID YOU KNOW?

Aquitaine is home to the Petit train d'Artouste, a seasonal narrow tourist railway that runs in the Pyrenees at an altitude of nearly 2,000 metres. It clings to the edge of the mountains, affording hair-raisingly incredible views.

REWARD
If you figured it out, you win one red train card.

FOR SOLUTION SEE PAGE 203

REVOLUTIONS

In the city of Marseille, you fall in with Jacques, a young train driver with an anti-authoritarian streak. As a station comes into view, your discussions surrounding the finer points of engine maintenance are interrupted when you notice a train sitting on the platform that prevents others from approaching.

"I'm early," Jacques says, looking at his watch, "but that train shouldn't be there."

To your surprise, and slight alarm, he does not slow down but accelerates towards the station, thankfully hitting the brakes hard, just inches from the platform.

"I'd better check in with the supervisor," he tells you gloomily and rushes off. The issue appears to be cleaned up smoothly, and when you later continue your journey, you enquire whether Jacques got into any trouble.

"Not at all!" he replies happily. "In fact I've been recommended for a promotion!"

Can you explain this turn of events?

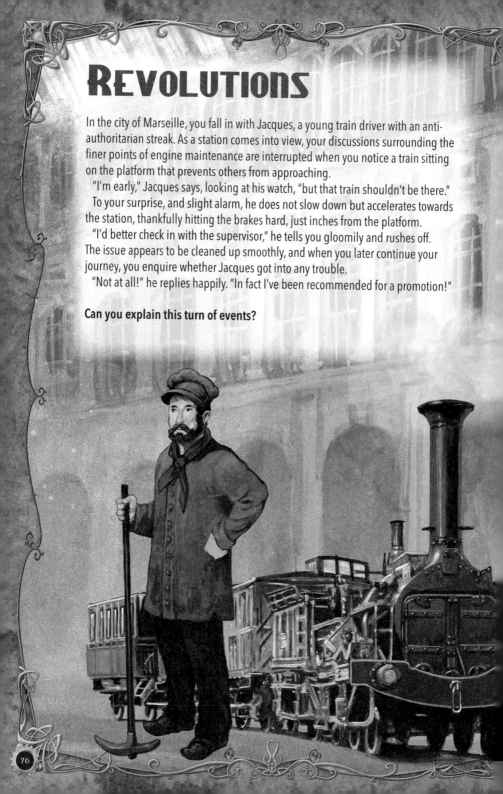

DID YOU KNOW?

Running from 1886 to 2003, Le Train Bleu was a legendary luxury sleeper train that ran all the way from Calais, through France, down to the resort towns of Nice and Monte Carlo. Both Poirot and Maigret solved mysteries set aboard the opulent express.

A funicular is available to save you climbing the hill of the Notre-Dame de la Garde in Marseille.

REWARD
If you figure it out, you win one white train card.

FOR SOLUTION SEE PAGE 203

JIGSAW JUMBLE

France has been kind to you, and you will leave it with many happy memories, a healthy wariness of bicycles and only a couple of extra pounds from the delicious food you've been treated to at every stop.

Your final stop is at the Palace of Versailles. This incredible château was the principal royal residence of France until 1789, and it has the architecture and grounds befitting of that honour. It has played its part in history already, with peace treaties and even the Proclamation of the German Empire – founding Germany as the modern nation it is today – being signed within its famed Hall of Mirrors. You are fortunate enough to have been offered a tour, and it takes you a whole day just to explore its gilded hallways.

Only two of the 12 jigsaw pieces fit into the picture below, while the rest have each been subtly changed.

Which two successfully complete the image?

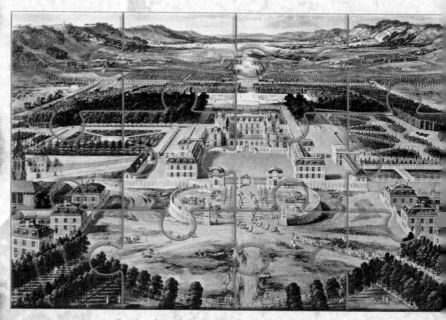

The Palace of Versailles as it looked during its first reconstruction in 1668.

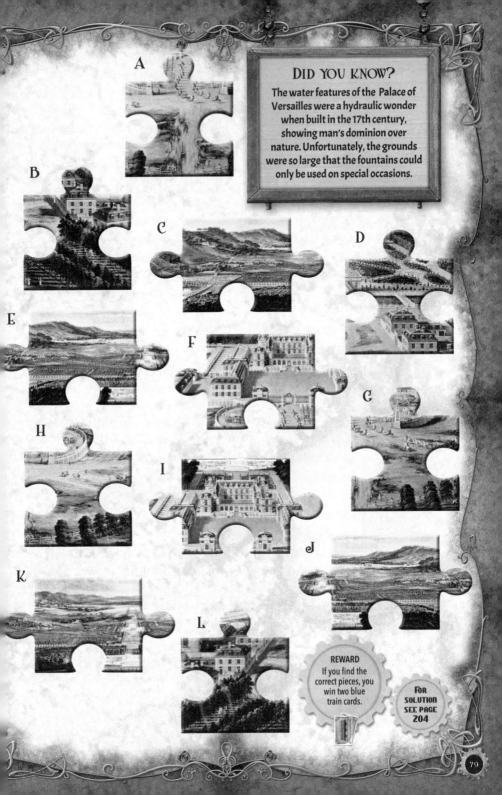

A

B

C

D

E

F

G

H

I

J

K

L

FOR SOLUTION SEE PAGE 204

DID YOU KNOW?
The water features of the Palace of Versailles were a hydraulic wonder when built in the 17th century, showing man's dominion over nature. Unfortunately, the grounds were so large that the fountains could only be used on special occasions.

REWARD
If you find the correct pieces, you win two blue train cards.

THE NETHERLANDS

The Low Countries (historically called the Netherlands) is a region on the coast of north-western Europe comprising Belgium, Luxembourg and parts of France and Germany, as well as the kingdom that retains the original moniker, the Netherlands.

The name is derived from the country's distinctive flat topography and low elevation. With 450 kilometres of coastline and more than a quarter of its land below sea level, water has always played a central role in the Netherlands' history, from maritime trade to massive land reclamation and the construction of its impressive canals.

The Netherlands is one of the continent's most densely populated countries. Its unique terrain reflects an equally unique culture, which attracts tourists from all over the world – of which you are now one!

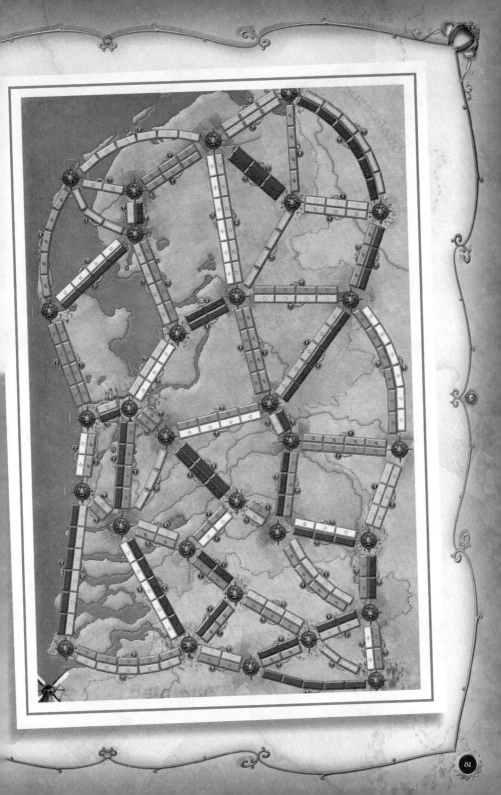

DISCOVER THE NETHERLANDS

You must have dozed off as you crossed the border, because a jolt of the train snaps you to consciousness and you're greeted with a riot of colour: the famous tulip fields of Holland! The reds, pinks and yellows flash pleasantly in front of your eyes, and you kick yourself for almost missing this lovely introduction to the country.

To make sure that you don't overlook anything else on your tour, you decide it is time to check out your guidebook. The names of 30 Dutch and Belgian cities (in Dutch or French) and one chain of islands are concealed in the grid opposite. They may run horizontally, vertically, diagonally, forward or backwards.

To make things more challenging, you must work out which cities are included by matching them with their facts below.

1.	Belgian city on the River Demer.	A_____
2.	Known as "The Venice of the North".	A_____
3.	Host of the 1920 Summer Olympics.	A_____
4.	Actual location of the bridge that inspired the film *A Bridge Too Far*.	A_____
5.	City's name means "Broad Aa", after one of its rivers.	B____
6.	Location of the Netherlands' main naval base.	D__ _____
7.	The Philips electronics company was founded here in 1891.	E_____
8.	Host of the first Women's Chess Olympiad in 1957.	E____
9.	City home to F.C. Twente and Europe's second-oldest marathon.	E_____
10.	Official name of government city known as "The Hague" in English.	'S _____
11.	City whose St Martin's Tower (Martinitoren) was twice destroyed by lightning	G_____
12.	Its name is believed to mean "elevated forest home".	H_____
13.	Location of Ethias, Belgium's largest arena.	H_____
14.	Birthplace of Hieronymus Bosch.	'S _____
15.	Frisian town with a leaning tower.	L_____
16.	City named after politician-engineer Cornelis Lely.	L_____
17.	Location of the Tour Paradis, the tallest skyscraper in Wallonia.	L____
18.	Capital of the province of Limburg.	M_____

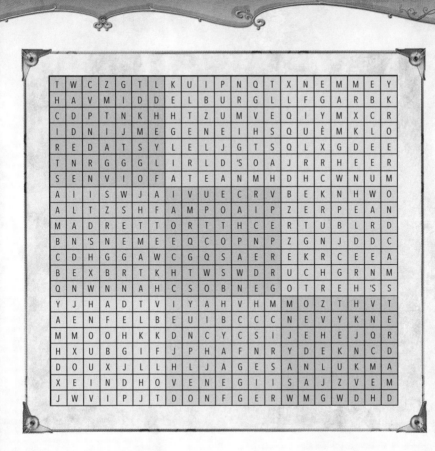

T	W	C	Z	G	T	L	K	U	I	P	N	Q	T	X	N	E	M	M	E	Y
H	A	V	M	I	D	D	E	L	B	U	R	G	L	L	F	G	A	R	B	K
C	D	P	T	N	K	H	H	T	Z	U	M	V	E	Q	I	Y	M	X	C	R
I	D	N	I	J	M	E	G	E	N	E	I	H	S	Q	U	È	M	K	L	O
R	E	D	A	T	S	Y	L	E	L	J	G	T	S	Q	L	X	G	D	E	E
T	N	R	G	G	G	L	I	R	L	D	'S	O	A	J	R	R	H	E	E	R
S	E	N	V	I	O	F	A	T	E	A	N	M	H	D	H	C	W	N	U	M
A	I	I	S	W	J	A	I	V	U	E	C	R	V	B	E	K	N	H	W	O
A	L	T	Z	S	H	F	A	M	P	O	A	I	P	Z	E	R	P	E	A	N
M	A	D	R	E	T	T	O	R	T	T	H	C	E	R	T	U	B	L	R	D
B	N	'S	N	E	M	E	E	Q	C	O	P	N	P	Z	G	N	J	D	D	C
C	D	H	G	G	A	W	C	G	Q	S	A	E	R	E	K	R	C	E	E	A
B	E	X	B	R	T	K	H	T	W	S	W	D	R	U	C	H	G	R	N	M
Q	N	W	N	N	A	H	C	S	O	B	N	E	G	O	T	R	E	H	'S	S
Y	J	H	A	D	T	V	I	Y	A	H	V	H	M	M	O	Z	T	H	V	T
A	E	N	F	E	L	B	E	U	I	B	C	C	C	N	E	V	Y	K	N	E
M	M	O	O	H	K	K	D	N	C	Y	C	S	I	J	E	H	E	J	Q	R
H	X	U	B	G	I	F	J	P	H	A	F	N	R	Y	D	E	K	N	C	D
D	O	U	X	J	L	L	H	L	J	A	G	E	S	A	N	L	U	K	M	A
X	E	I	N	D	H	O	V	E	N	E	G	I	I	S	A	J	Z	V	E	M
J	W	V	I	P	J	T	D	O	N	F	G	E	R	W	M	G	W	D	H	D

19. Capital of the province of Zeeland. M_____
20. Believed by many to be the oldest city of the Netherlands. N_____
21. Epicentre of a significant earthquake in 1992. R_____
22. Europe's largest seaport. R_____
23. Famous for its Waterpoort gate. S_____
24. Home of Cartamundi playing cards since 1970. T_____
25. Location of the Netherlands' busiest railway station. U_____
26. The West Frisian Islands. W_____
27. This city's inhabitants are sometimes called "Bluefingers". Z_____

REWARD
You win two white train cards for correctly identifying and finding half of all of the cities and another two if you can find them all.

FOR SOLUTION SEE PAGE 205

MAKE TRACKS

Antwerp is a historic and wealthy city, with beautiful architecture and a world-famous diamond district that is the hub of the world's diamond trade. As much as you admire the jewellery on show, you have your mind set on a different sort of diamond – the Antwerp Central railway station. Unfortunately, it is still a couple of years away from completion, but architects are already describing it as the most beautiful rail station in the world, and as you stand in its vast shadow you can see why.

You take a seat nearby where you can watch the construction workers busying themselves around the site, and imagine the millions of adventures that will shortly begin from this magnificent building. To pass the time, you turn to your semi-complete puzzle book.

Can you design a railway that connects all of the stations and rail yards?
Draw a single continuous line around the grid that passes through every station and rail yard.

If the line enters a station, turn left or right within its square before passing straight through the next square you come to. Ensure that this works for both routes going in and out of the station.

If the line enters a rail yard, keep going straight through its square before turning left or right in the next square. Ensure that this works for at least one route going into the rail yard.

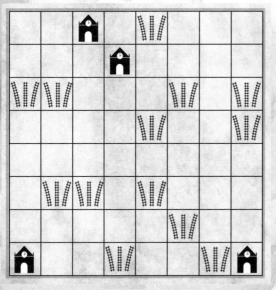

KEY

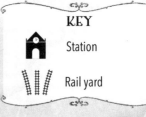

Station

Rail yard

REWARD
If you successfully connect all the stations and yards, you win two black train cards.

FOR SOLUTION SEE PAGE 205

A FULSOME POPE

One slight difficulty that you have encountered on your journeys around the Low Countries has been the language barrier – or languages barrier, you should say. The region is home to so many dialects – from Flemish and Dutch to French and German, via Luxembourgish, Frisian, Walloon, Picard, Tweants, Achterhooks and more – that often it is hard enough to recognise the language being spoken, let alone the meaning! Nevertheless, everyone is so friendly and helpful that you always manage to make yourself understood in the end.

One conversation was so perplexing that you transcribed certain key words as best you could. The following list of anagrams are things connected to the Netherlands and Belgium. They all have something in common and there is a clue in the title, which is also an anagram.

Can you unscramble the anagrams and say what binds them together?

1.	**TV CHANGING OVEN**
2.	**A WAGON MOLLIFIER**
3.	**HAM TIARA**
4.	**DEADLINE HAVEN**
5.	**AQUILINE HEN MEWL**
6.	**CHURN JAY OFF**
7.	**URETHRA URGE**
8.	**JENS FAME SANK**
9.	**MANMADE VEALED CAJUN**
10.	**PURER HYENA BUD**

REWARD
If you discover the connection, you win one green train card, and for unscrambling all the names you win an additional green train card.

FOR SOLUTION SEE PAGE 206

GOING DUTCH

Your time is limited, and you want to see as much as possible, so it's time for a whirlwind tour of the Netherlands. You make a plan to visit five locations in just five days! Each day you are accompanied by a different travelling companion that you have already met on your journey, and who has invited you to visit them in order to see something quintessentially (or stereotypically) Dutch.

At the end of it all, you finally find time to sit down and write it up in your journal. Can you put together the events of one of your most eventful weeks? You decide to put a time limit on yourself, to match the swift pace of your sightseeing.

Can you fill in all the facts from the memories below?

1. You bought some traditional wooden clogs on Wednesday; two days earlier you had been in Zwolle but not with Beau.

2. Alex was your companion the day after you saw an impressive collection of windmills and the day before you went to Groningen.

3. You travelled with Dani on Thursday, but you didn't see the tulips together and you definitely didn't see those magnificent flowers in Rotterdam.

4. The taste of cheese will forever be associated in your mind with the city of Haarlem. The cheese shop experience was only surpassed by your picturesque canal adventure with Chris.

Day	Companion	Location	Activity
Monday			
Tuesday			
Wednesday			
Thursday			
Friday			

	Alex	Beau	Chris	Dani	Elian	Haarlem	Groningen	Amsterdam	Zwolle	Rotterdam	Canal trip	Tulips	Clogs	Windmills	Cheese shop
Monday															
Tuesday															
Wednesday															
Thursday															
Friday															
Canal trip															
Tulips															
Clogs															
Windmills															
Cheese shop															
Haarlem															
Groningen															
Amsterdam															
Zwolle															
Rotterdam															

ROTTERDAM TO AMSTERDAM

The sights of Amsterdam in the midst of its second Golden Age have been wonderful, and the Dutch pancakes even more so. You have spent much of your visit wandering the busy canals, listening to the Royal Orchestra perform in the new concert hall and examining priceless artworks in the Rijksmuseum (Rembrandt has always been a particular favourite of yours), but in your spare time the pancakes have been too much of a delicious temptation.

As a consequence, you think it's time for a workout. Watching the denizens of the city cycle so elegantly to-and-fro has given you the courage for another try on a bicycle, and so you borrow one for a day trip to Ouderkerk aan de Amstel, a charmingly quaint 12th century village a few miles out of the city. This attempt was far more successful than your last, and you spend a peaceful day being shown around by a young train enthusiast who wants to hear about your rail adventures just as much as you want to learn about his village.

In order to recount your journey to him, you must work out your route and insert the tracks into the grid below.

The numbers on the periphery tell you how many rail sections must be in that row or column, although some numbers are missing to make things harder.

You may place only a straight or a curved section inside a box. The tracks cannot cross themselves.

Straight

Curve

Can you connect Rotterdam to Amsterdam?

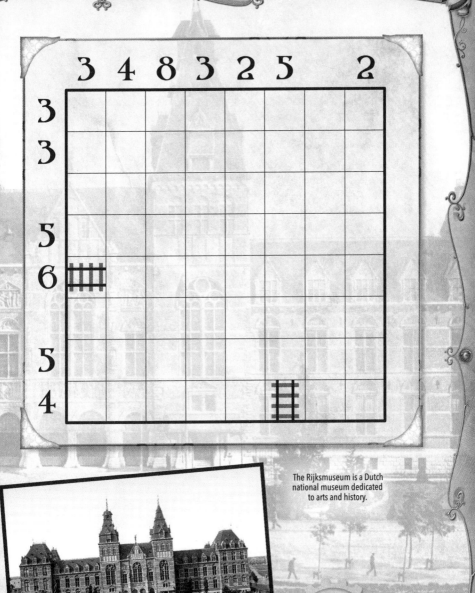

The Rijksmuseum is a Dutch national museum dedicated to arts and history.

REWARD
If you recount your journey successfully, you win two purple train cards.

FOR SOLUTION SEE PAGE 206

Mondrian-Esque

The Netherlands have produced numerous master artists, and while you were in Amsterdam you were pleased to come across the work of a little-known artist who had died some years previously, but had painted a series of works that you particularly enjoyed. There was something about the sunflowers that drew you to them every time you glanced at them, and you had been so taken with them that you had managed to find space in your luggage for one of the paintings. You plan to hang it in your living room when your long tour is finally over.

Now you have arrived at the city of Amersfoort, which has one of the Netherland's largest railway junctions (the new central railway station has just opened) and is where you meet a young teacher currently called Piet Mondriaan, who takes you to his studio where he is working on some of his own paintings. You come across one, half-finished, but clearly an exploration of geometric forms and primary colours that he calls *Composition with Red Blue and Yellow*. It's certainly unusual, but you are quite taken with it.

The sequence opposite is influenced by this painting and follows a predictable pattern.

Can you determine what should come next?

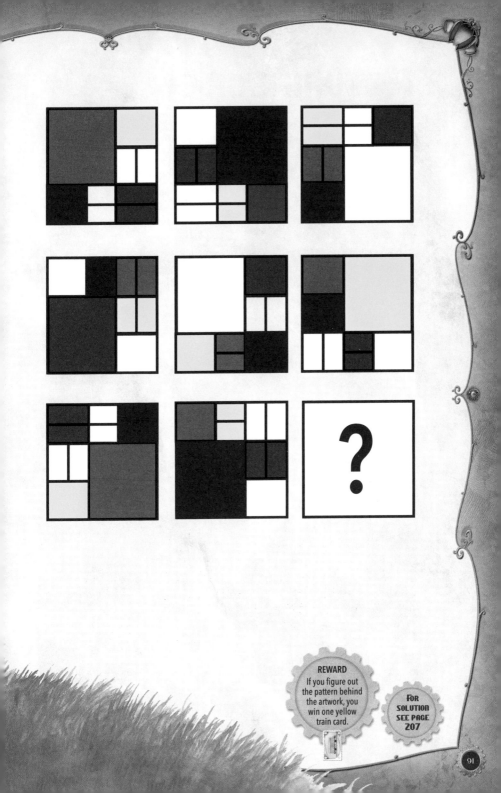

REWARD
If you figure out the pattern behind the artwork, you win one yellow train card.

FOR SOLUTION SEE PAGE 207

RETURN TICKET

A return visit to Brussels is next on your itinerary. Your train sets out from Antwerp at 9.25 am on Monday morning and arrives in Brussels 41 minutes later.

You spend a happy week of intensive sightseeing, with particular highlights being the time spent exploring the Grand Place and its surrounding buildings, and getting completely lost in the Palace of Justice – rumoured to be the largest building constructed in the last century, which you can attest to. It took you an hour just to find the exit!

You eventually make the journey back to Antwerp from the Belgian capital. Your train departs at 9.24 am, following the same line that brought you to Brussels and arriving back at 10.05 am.

During your return journey, would there be any point along the route where you are in the same place at exactly the same time as on your outbound journey?

Can you explain your conclusion?

The Grande Place in Brussels,
which took you a whole day
to explore.

DID YOU KNOW?

The first railway in continental Europe opened on 5 May 1835 between Brussels and Mechelen. The design emulated the British railway, which is why Belgian trains "drive" on the left (like British cars), while Belgian cars drive on the right.

REWARD
If you figure it out, you win one red train card.

FOR SOLUTION SEE PAGE 207

POLDERS

The guidebook had told you about how flat and "low" the Netherlands was, but seeing the completely smooth countryside roll out in front of your train window, without a hill in sight, is still quite something.

On the train from Zwolle to Emmen, you had been musing about this for some time when a fellow traveller sits opposite you and you begin to make polite conversation. It is just your astounding good fortune to learn that he is an engineer!

"You see, almost a fifth of the Netherlands has been reclaimed from the sea by an ingenious system called empoldering," he explained. "A dyke is constructed around an area of land to prevent more water flooding in, then the area is drained and fertilized. It can take over a decade to turn the area into a polder that is ready to grow crops and be built upon, but we are a patient people. It is no matter."

He begins to sketch an example for you. Can you divide the land below into four equal parts with exactly the same shape and surface area?

Dykes in the Netherlands in the 19th century.

REWARD
If you figure it out, you win one blue train card.

FOR SOLUTION SEE PAGE 207

Windmills

The friendly engineer is impressed with your empoldering skills, so he moves on to another famed Dutch engineering masterpiece: the windmill.

"Harnessing clean, natural energy is not a new concept in the Netherlands. With its predominantly flat terrain, it is not surprising to me that the windmill has become a Dutch icon – when out in the countryside, you see them in almost every direction you turn!"

He continued, with a twinkle in his eye: "Windmills are mainly used to pump water out of the lowlands to create polders, as well as to power lumber saws and grind grain. Here, let me set you another challenge to see just how Dutch you are."

Can you separate each of the nine windmills below from one another by drawing just two squares? The train is only five minutes from Emmen, so think fast!

REWARD
If you successfully draw the two squares before the train pulls in to Emmen, you win three orange train cards. If it takes longer, you win one orange train card.

FOR SOLUTION SEE PAGE 208

ALL CHANGE!

Your tour has been eventful. You have examined paintings, learned about engineering marvels, seen glorious architecture and spent time appreciating all the colours of the many varieties of Dutch tulips. And eaten more than your own weight in pancakes… not to mention the cheese. It's time to move on before you start to struggle to fit through the train doors!

   Before you leave, you commission two postcards from a street artist to commemorate the people you have met on your travels. However, as your train pulls out from the station you notice that something is not quite right about them.

Can you find the 12 differences between the picture on the left and the one on the right?

DID YOU KNOW?

The Netherlands is famous for its traditional windmills, and there are over 1,000 scattered around the land. The Dutch love of wind energy extends to trains too. The rail network is completely electric and runs 100% on renewable energy.

REWARD
If you find all 12 differences, you win two orange train cards.

FOR SOLUTION SEE PAGE 208

ITALY

The Kingdom of Italy was established just four decades ago, in 1861. However, the states that comprise the nation are considerably older and have had a profound influence on the history of Europe.

The city of Rome was founded in 753 BCE. Initially a monarchy, it later became a republic and then rose to become the epicentre of a mighty empire that dominated most of the continent. It was also instrumental in establishing Christianity as a world religion and became the seat of ecclesiastical power.

The Renaissance flourished in Florence in the fourteenth century, and during this period Italy was transformed into a centre of culture and science. Its proud traditions of art and architecture, haute couture and cutting-edge technology continue to this day.

DISCOVER ITALY

Travelling south through the Fréjus Rail Tunnel, (you are slowly getting used to chugging underneath mountains) you are surprised to learn just how new Italy is as a country, given the fame of the Roman Empire and how influential Rome and Italy have been in cultural, scientific and religious developments throughout modern history. Your first stop is in Turin, which was the initial capital city of the nascent Italy in the 1860s.

Wandering the sunny piazzas, you hear a sudden beeping and have to leap out of the way as an automobile races past. A young man joins you as you watch it disappear into the distance.

"That's a new Fiat 4 HP. Isn't it *fantastico*?" He sighs, with unconcealed envy. "They make them here, in Turin. It can race at 35 kilometres per hour. It is scarcely believable, no?"

You agree that it is a marvel, though you wish the driver had given you a little more warning. Taking a moment to calm down, you settle down in front of the Palazzo Madama to plan your route around Italy, before later exploring its Royal Art Gallery.

The names of 33 Italian cities (in Italian) are concealed in the grid opposite. They may run horizontally, vertically, diagonally, forward or backwards. To make things more challenging, you must work out which cities are included by matching them with the facts below.

1.	Location of the archaeological site Valle dei Templi (Valley of the Temples).	A_____
2.	The city's name is derived from the Greek word for "elbow".	A_____
3.	A coastal city with a long tradition of consuming raw fish.	B___
4.	A funicular railway connects its upper city to its lower city.	B_____
5.	The oldest European university was built here in 1088.	B_____
6.	Alpine capital of South Tyrol.	B_____
7.	Capital of the island of Sardinia.	C_____
8.	Second largest city in Sicily; it has a view of Mount Etna.	C_____
9.	Final resting place of Alaric, first king of the Visigoths.	C_____
10.	Birthplace of Dante Alighieri and Florence Nightingale.	F_____
11.	South-eastern agricultural city, largely rebuilt after an earthquake in 1731.	F_____
12.	Birthplace of Christopher Columbus.	G_____
13.	City surrounded by fortified Medicean Walls.	G_____
14.	Nicknamed "The Florence of the South".	L____
15.	Sicilian port city named Ζάγκλη ("scythe") by its Greek founders.	M_____
16.	Capital of Lombardy, famous for finance, fashion and football.	M_____
17.	Birthplace of the modern pizza.	N_____
18.	Main connection between the island of Sardinia and the Italian peninsula.	O____
19.	Home to Italy's largest opera house, the Teatro Massimo.	P_____
20.	Northern city, famous for its dry-cured ham (prosciutto).	P____
21.	Capital of the Umbria region, famous for its chocolate.	P_____

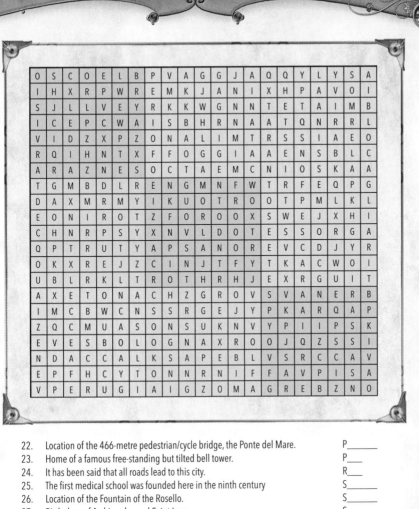

```
O S C O E L B P V A G G J A Q Q Y L Y S A
I H X R P W R E M K J A N I X H P A V O I
S J L L V E Y R K K W G N N T E T A I M B
I C E P C W A I S B H R N A A T Q N R R L
V I D Z X P Z O N A L I M T R S S I A E O
R Q I H N T X F F O G G I A A E N S B L C
A R A Z N E S O C T A E M C N I O S K A A
T G M B D L R E N G M N F W T R F E Q P A
D A X M R M Y I K U O T R O O T P M L K L
E O N I R O T Z F O R O O X S W E J X H I
C H N R P S Y X N V L D O T E S S O R G A
Q P T R U T Y A P S A N O R E V C D J Y R
O K X R E J Z C I N J T F Y T K A C W O I
U B L R K L T R O T H R H J E X R G U I T
A X E T O N A C H Z G R O V S V A N E R B
I M C B W C N S S R G E J Y P K A R Q A P
Z Q C M U A S O N S U K N V V Y P I I P S K
E V E S B O L O G N A X R O O J Q Z S S I
N D A C C A L K S A P E B L V S R C C A V
E P F H C Y T O N N R N I F F A V P I S A
V P E R U G I A I G Z O M A G R E B Z N O
```

22. Location of the 466-metre pedestrian/cycle bridge, the Ponte del Mare.   P_____
23. Home of a famous free-standing but tilted bell tower.   P___
24. It has been said that all roads lead to this city.   R___
25. The first medical school was founded here in the ninth century   S_____
26. Location of the Fountain of the Rosello.   S_____
27. Birthplace of Archimedes and Saint Lucy.   S_____
28. Apulian coastal city founded by the Spartans in the eighth century BCE.   T_____
29. North-eastern town on the borders of Austria and Slovenia.   T_____
30. Capital of the Kingdom of Italy between 1861 and 1865.   T_____
31. North-eastern seaport that belonged to Austria between 1382 and the end of WWI. T_____
32. The city was a republic known as La Serenissima between 697 and 1797.   V_____
33. Shakespeare's Romeo and Juliet is set in this city.   V_____

REWARD
You win two blue train cards for correctly identifying and finding half of the towns and cities and another two if you can find them all.

FOR SOLUTION SEE PAGE 209

MAKE TRACKS

The sea is calling you, and so you catch the train to Genoa, which you have heard has both a maze of beautiful palaces and piazzas, and historic seaside districts such as the Boccadesse, a colourful and ancient mariners' village. The train is just 10 minutes from arrival, and you decide to challenge yourself with your puzzle book.

Can you design a railway that connects all of the stations and rail yards before you arrive at Genoa?
Draw a single continuous line around the grid that passes through every station and rail yard.

If the line enters a station, turn left or right within its square before passing straight through the next square you come to. Ensure that this works for both routes going in and out of the station.

If the line enters a rail yard, keep going straight through its square before turning left or right in the next square. Ensure that this works for at least one route going into the rail yard.

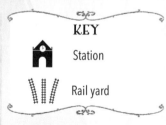

KEY

🏠 Station

▨ Rail yard

FOR SOLUTION SEE PAGE 209

Sad Abs Unform

Jumbling up your journey keeps you on your toes, and gives you more time to ride your favourite trains and take in the incredible Italian countryside. You therefore take a long train south to Naples, where you disembark and head even further south to explore something truly unique: the ongoing excavations at Pompeii.

This ancient Roman city was buried in 79 AD, and major excavations are currently taking place to uncover this historical goldmine. You are fortunate enough to secure a tour with the lead archaeologist, who shows you newly-discovered jewellery, vases, statues and slabs of writing that expose the workings of everyday Roman life. Much of his time is spent painstakingly piecing these items back together again, and he sets you a task to see if you could be of help.

The following list of anagrams are things connected to Italy, including from the twentieth century to come. They all have something in common and there is a clue in the title, which is also an anagram.

Can you unscramble the anagrams and say what binds them together?

1.	ALOOF MARE	
2.	ABANDON BAG DECAL	
3.	RARE FIR	
4.	AN ORIGAMI IGOR	
5.	BROILING HAM	
6.	MINI RAT	
7.	AIRSTEAM	
8.	ROPE IN	
9.	ILL PIER	
10.	AD RAP	
11.	EVES CAR	

REWARD
If you unscramble all the names, you win two yellow train cards.

FOR SOLUTION SEE PAGE 210

MYSTERIES OF THE TAROT

During your time in Milan you visit a fortune teller, drawn to her by the beautiful hand-painted cards she uses in her divinations. She tells you that tarot cards may have originated from the city in the fifteenth century, and some of the earliest and most beautiful decks were created right in that very city.

Looking deep into your eyes, she declares: "You are a traveller who chases after enigmas."

You confirm the truth of her words but profess no interest in knowing your fate – exploration and discovery are all about journeying into the unknown.

The fortune teller removes the Major Arcana cards from her deck – that is, those with names such as "Death" and "The Lovers" – until she is left holding 56 cards comprising four suits (Swords, Coins, Wands and Cups) which are divided into 14 ranks (Ace to 10 plus a Jack, Knight, Queen and King). She shuffles the deck and place three cards onto the table, face down.

"Then I have a puzzle for you," she says. "What are the faces of these three cards?"

You politely explain that being an ace puzzle solver does not make you a clairvoyant.

She smiles, "I shall give you four clues…"

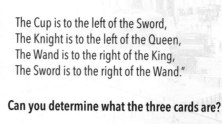

The Cup is to the left of the Sword,
The Knight is to the left of the Queen,
The Wand is to the right of the King,
The Sword is to the right of the Wand."

Can you determine what the three cards are?

The Duomo di Milano is still being built in 1900, having been started in 1386.

VICHY

REWARD
If you work it out, you win three black train cards.

FOR SOLUTION SEE PAGE 210

VERONA TO VENICE

As a lover of culture, you are thrilled to be standing beneath a medieval balcony in Verona, purported to be Juliet's own balcony from where the star-crossed lover was won over by Romeo's wooing. Of course, she wasn't real, and this is just an attractive medieval balcony… but you can't help but be touched by the romanticism of the moment. A young man with a traveller's bag breaks your reverie.

"The fair city of Verona is wonderful, is it not? There is something special in the air here. But Venice… have you been?"

You tell him you have not, but hope to soon.

"This is a disaster! You cannot truly understand romance and passion until you have glided down its glistening canals by starlight. Come, come, I am on my way there now. Will you travel with me?"

The man's enthusiasm is so infectious that you find yourself agreeing before you have even considered your travel plans.

For your journey, you must work out the correct route and insert the tracks into the grid below. The numbers on the periphery tell you how many rail sections must be in that row or column, but unnumbered rows and columns may also have rail sections.

You may only place a straight or a curved section inside a box. The tracks cannot cross themselves.

Straight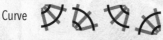

Curve

Can you connect Verona to Venice?

A view of a stone bridge crossing the Adige in Verona.

	1		2		3	3	
7							
6							
4							
4							
2							

Your gondola approaching you on the Grand Canal in Venice.

REWARD
If you find your way to your destination, you win two multi-coloured train cards.

FOR SOLUTION SEE PAGE 211

PISA

After spending a delightful week among the waterways of Venice, you travel cross-country to visit the city of Pisa, which is famous for its iconic leaning tower as well as being the birthplace of Leonardo Bonacci, one of the greatest mathematicians of the Middle Ages.

The University of Pisa was founded in 1343 and has some very distinguished alumni, including no fewer than five popes. Your visit to its faculty brings you into contact with some fellow puzzle solvers, and you spend a merry few hours exchanging riddles and conundrums of all types with them.

"Here's an easy puzzle with some local flavour," chuckles a student, while writing letters onto an old chalkboard.

If the top row is a sequence, what should come next on the bottom row?

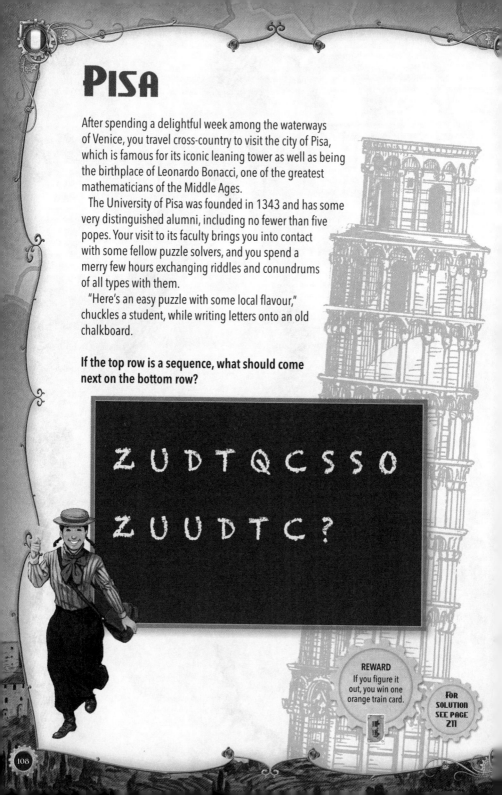

Z U D T Q C S S O

Z U U D T C ?

REWARD
If you figure it out, you win one orange train card.

FOR SOLUTION SEE PAGE 211

FIVE TO FOUR

The good fortune you have experienced on your travels continues. A fellow passenger is returning to Vatican City and agrees to share his knowledge with you on a lengthy tour. As you admire the Renaissance architecture, you discover another stroke of luck: it becomes apparent that he shares your love of enigmas and mysteries.

In between histories of the artworks and sculptures that seem to cover pretty much every surface, you discuss how Latin has influenced the grammar and lexicons of many of Europe's languages. Your friend demonstrates the similarities and differences by focusing on the number "5" as it is written in ten languages.

He cannot resist giving you a puzzle to see if your lateral thinking is on a par with your linguistic skills. He asks you:

"In which of these languages can you get four from five by taking two?"

Czech	pĕt
Danish	fem
Dutch	vijf
English	five
French	cinq
German	fünf
Greek	πέντε
Italian	cinque
Lithuanian	penki
Spanish	cinco

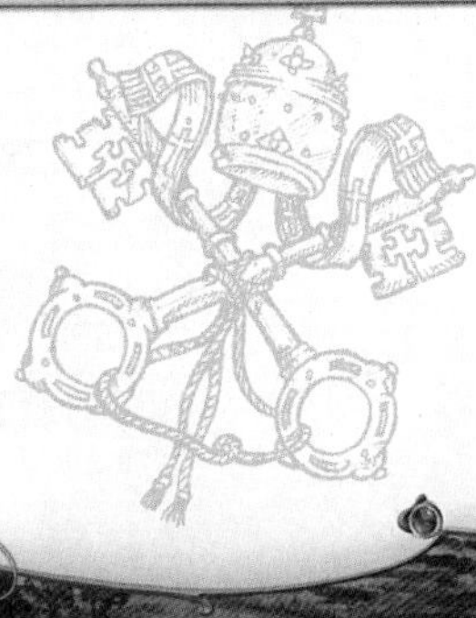

REWARD
If you figure it out, you win one white train card.

FOR SOLUTION SEE PAGE 211

TUSCANY

You decide to take some time to simply enjoy the beautiful landscape of Tuscany by steam locomotive. This area was the birthplace of the Italian Renaissance and has understandably become a tourist magnet, with its beautiful beaches, prolific vineyards and sites of incredible Italian heritage, such as the Medici villas.

As you criss-cross the countryside, taking in the sights through the train windows and occasionally alighting to stretch your legs in one stunning rural village after another, you decide to occupy yourself with some mental challenges. Your recent trip to Pisa has given you a taste for arithmetical conundrums, so you jot the following into your journal:

On the outbound excursion, the train averaged 50 kilometres per hour for the first half of the journey and 66 kilometres per hour for the remainder.

On the return, the train made a constant 57 kilometres per hour.

Which journey was the fastest?

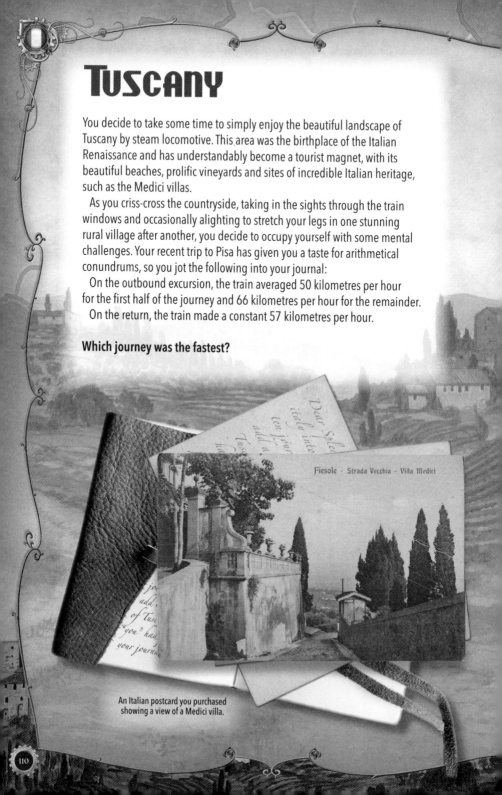

An Italian postcard you purchased showing a view of a Medici villa.

REWARD
If you figure it
out, you win one
red train card.

FOR SOLUTION SEE PAGE 211

RENAISSANCE GRAFFITI

Out in the countryside, you find yourself enjoying the slower pace of life, and end up staying a number of nights in a rural farmhouse in the region surrounding Florence. While there, you take the opportunity to visit a number of glorious old monasteries, learning about the lives of the monks who once lived there.

You decide that their pace of life was a little too slow for you, but there's no doubting their importance to the cultural and scientific growth of humankind over the years. You particularly enjoy learning about the monks of the Cistercian Order, who created an ingenious number system. Unlike Roman and Arabic numerals, your farmhouse host explains, each number from 1 to 9,999 is represented by a single symbol. Below are the numbers 1 to 12. Can you see how 11 relates to 10 and 1?

Noting your fascination, on one particularly fine morning your host guides you to an ancient church, in which you find these symbols etched into the masonry. It looks like a piece of sixteenth-century graffiti!

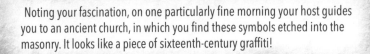

Who might have inscribed this Renaissance era tag?

REWARD
If you work it out, you win one purple train card.

FOR SOLUTION SEE PAGE 212

JIGSAW JUMBLE

To finish your Italian tour, you sail to Sicily, the largest island in the Mediterranean and home to Mount Etna, the tallest active volcano in Europe. Although fascinated by the idea of witnessing a volcanic eruption, you are quite happy to learn that there hasn't been any geologic activity to speak of recently. Instead, you take up residence briefly in Palermo, where you discover another beautiful Italian cathedral to add to your list.

This particular cathedral was first built in 1185, but has been added to bit by bit over the years (it was only completed at the end of the 18th century) giving it an interesting appearance of a mixture of different styles. Outside, you are stopped by a jigsaw-seller with an unusual conundrum for you. Just as the architecture is something of a jumble, so is his jigsaw.

You only have a few minutes before your boat departs for the mainland. Nine of the jigsaw pieces on the right fit into the picture below, but three of them do not.

Which are the odd ones out, and can you find them in the three minutes you have before you need to rush to your ship?

An engraving of Palermo Cathedral.

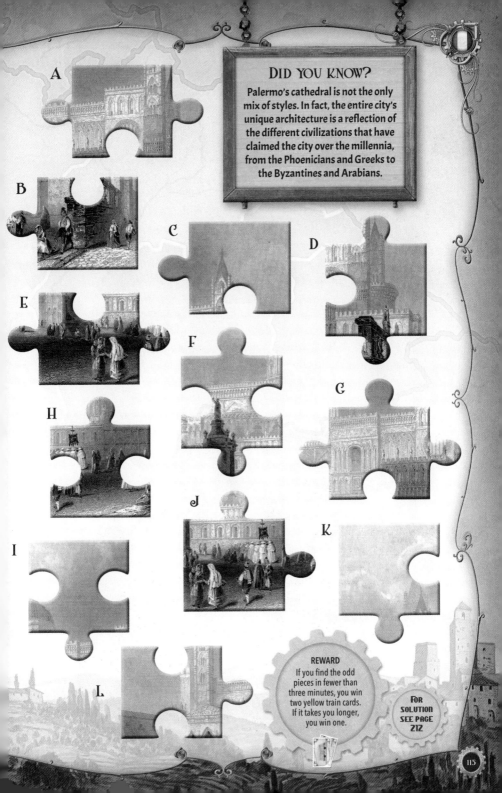

A

B

C

D

E

F

G

H

I

J

K

L

DID YOU KNOW?

Palermo's cathedral is not the only mix of styles. In fact, the entire city's unique architecture is a reflection of the different civilizations that have claimed the city over the millennia, from the Phoenicians and Greeks to the Byzantines and Arabians.

REWARD
If you find the odd pieces in fewer than three minutes, you win two yellow train cards. If it takes you longer, you win one.

FOR SOLUTION SEE PAGE 212

THE BRITISH ISLES

Off the north-west coast of Europe lies a group of islands whose eclectic history has been defined both by its continental neighbours and by more distant lands from its time as the seat of a globe-spanning empire. The resultant cultural diversity has created a remarkable patchwork of countries (England, Scotland, Ireland and Wales) and distinct regions such as Merseyside, Cornwall, the Scottish Highlands and Ulster.

Great Britain was also at the heart of the Industrial Revolution. The first steam train prototype was produced by Scots inventor William Murdoch in 1784 and the first working railway locomotive built by Cornish engineer Richard Trevithick in 1804. The country has the world's oldest railway system which opened to the public in 1825.

There is no better way to enjoy Britain's cornucopia of regional customs, dialects and landscape than by rail, and you plan on starting that exploration now.

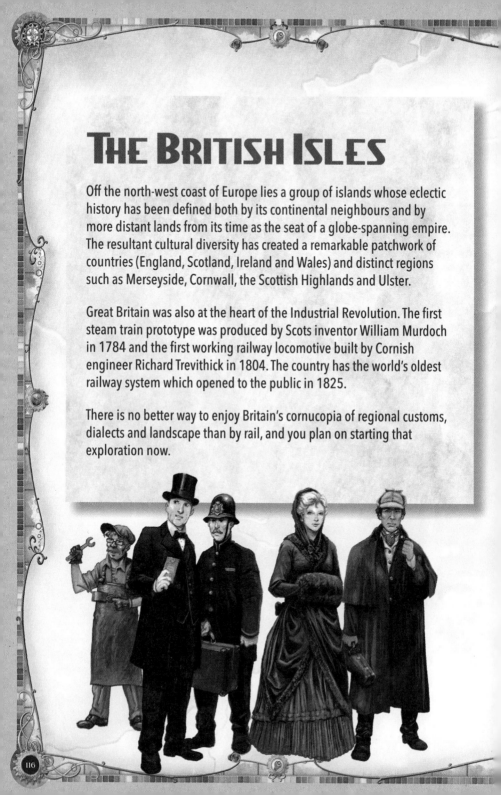

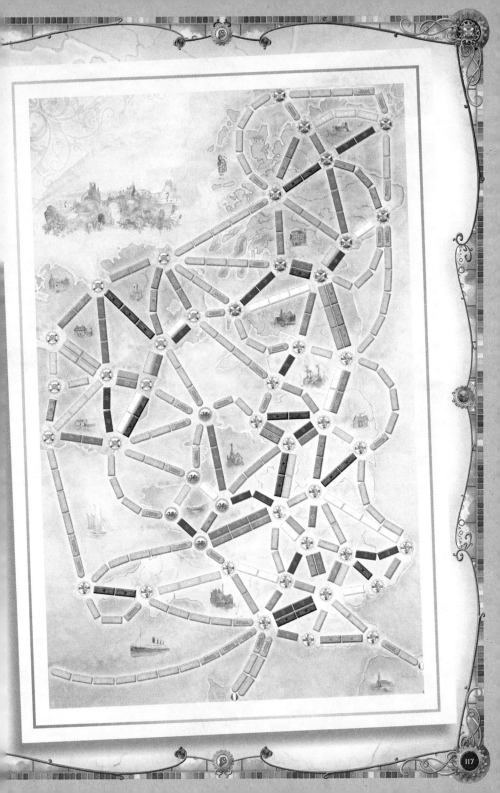

DISCOVER THE BRITISH ISLES

While crossing the English Channel from continental Europe, the iconic White Cliffs of Dover finally come into view. Your authentic British welcome is made complete when your ferry pulls into the fog-laden port and it starts to rain. The locals seem to shrug off the steady drizzle without a second thought, so you determine to do the same.

You gather up your luggage – a task made more difficult by the souvenirs you are collecting on your wanderings – walk to a local tea room, pull out your guide, and start making your plans. The names of 42 towns and cities are concealed in the grid opposite. They may run horizontally, vertically, diagonally, forward or backwards.

To make things more challenging, you must work out which cities are included by matching them with their facts below.

1.	Scottish city noted for its sparkly local granite.	A_____
2.	Seaside town on Cardigan Bay.	A_____
3.	Birthplace of C. S. Lewis and Van Morrison.	B_____
4.	Home of the Bull Ring shopping centre and the Spaghetti Junction.	B_____
5.	Seaside city where you can see the Palace Pier and Royal Pavilion.	B_____
6.	The Temple Meads railway station opened here in 1840.	B_____
7.	University city that lies to the south of the Fens.	C_____
8.	Became a city in 1905 and a capital in 1955.	C_____
9.	County seat of Cumbria.	C_____
10.	The island of Ireland's third largest city.	C___
11.	Coastal town famous for its chalk cliffs.	D____
12.	City on the River Liffey, also called Baile Átha Cliath.	D_____
13.	This town's motto is "I gave birth to brave Cú Chulainn".	D_____
14.	Location of the Mills Observatory built in 1935.	D____
15.	Home of the Palace of Holyroodhouse and the Scottish National Gallery.	E_____
16.	Highland town on the shore of Loch Linnhe.	F___ _____
17.	Connacht's "City of the Tribes".	G_____
18.	Home to the world's third oldest underground rail network.	G_____
19.	Anglesey seaport serving Wales and Ireland.	H_____
20.	King Charles I failed to capture this city in 1642.	H___
21.	Principal city of the Highlands and the Great Glen.	I_____
22.	County seat of Suffolk.	I_____
23.	Largest city in West Yorkshire.	L____
24.	Primary setting of the 1996 memoir and 1999 film *Angela's Ashes*.	L_____
25.	Location of the Goodison Park and Anfield football grounds.	L_____
26.	Spa town and administrative centre of Powys.	L_____ _____
27.	Location of Shakespeare's Globe theatre.	L_____
28.	Home of the world's oldest surviving rail station.	M_____
29.	City linked to Gateshead by the Tyne Bridge.	N_____
30.	Its historic castle was destroyed to create a railway station in 1879.	N_____

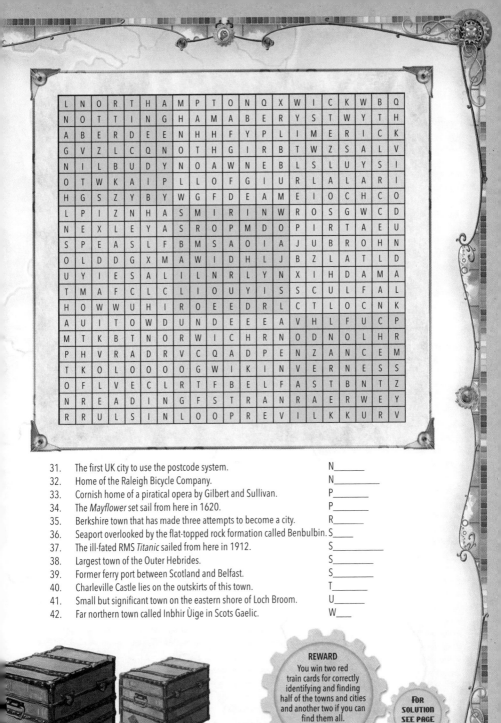

L	N	O	R	T	H	A	M	P	T	O	N	Q	X	W	I	C	K	W	B	Q
N	O	T	T	I	N	G	H	A	M	A	B	E	R	Y	S	T	W	Y	T	H
A	B	E	R	D	E	E	N	H	H	F	Y	P	L	I	M	E	R	I	C	K
G	V	Z	L	C	Q	N	O	T	H	G	I	R	B	T	W	Z	S	A	L	V
N	I	L	B	U	D	Y	N	O	A	W	N	E	B	L	S	L	U	Y	S	I
O	T	W	K	A	I	P	L	L	O	F	G	I	U	R	L	A	L	A	R	I
H	G	S	Z	Y	B	Y	W	G	F	D	E	A	M	E	I	O	C	H	C	O
L	P	I	Z	N	H	A	S	M	I	R	I	N	W	R	O	S	G	W	C	D
N	E	X	L	E	Y	A	S	R	O	P	M	D	O	P	I	R	T	A	E	U
S	P	E	A	S	L	F	B	M	S	A	O	I	A	J	U	B	R	O	H	N
O	L	D	D	G	X	M	A	W	I	D	H	L	J	B	Z	L	A	T	L	D
U	Y	I	E	S	A	L	I	L	N	R	L	Y	N	X	I	H	D	A	M	A
T	M	A	F	C	L	C	L	I	O	U	Y	I	S	S	C	U	L	F	A	L
H	O	W	W	U	H	I	R	O	E	E	D	R	L	C	T	L	O	C	N	K
A	U	I	T	O	W	D	U	N	D	E	E	E	A	V	H	L	F	U	C	P
M	T	K	B	T	N	O	R	W	I	C	H	R	N	O	D	N	O	L	H	R
P	H	V	R	A	D	R	V	C	Q	A	D	P	E	N	Z	A	N	C	E	M
T	K	O	L	O	O	O	O	G	W	I	K	I	N	V	E	R	N	E	S	S
O	F	L	V	E	C	L	R	T	F	B	E	L	F	A	S	T	B	N	T	Z
N	R	E	A	D	I	N	G	F	S	T	R	A	N	R	A	E	R	W	E	W
R	R	U	L	S	I	N	L	O	O	P	R	E	V	I	L	K	K	U	R	V

31. The first UK city to use the postcode system. N_____
32. Home of the Raleigh Bicycle Company. N_____
33. Cornish home of a piratical opera by Gilbert and Sullivan. P_____
34. The *Mayflower* set sail from here in 1620. P_____
35. Berkshire town that has made three attempts to become a city. R_____
36. Seaport overlooked by the flat-topped rock formation called Benbulbin. S____
37. The ill-fated RMS *Titanic* sailed from here in 1912. S_____
38. Largest town of the Outer Hebrides. S_____
39. Former ferry port between Scotland and Belfast. S_____
40. Charleville Castle lies on the outskirts of this town. T_____
41. Small but significant town on the eastern shore of Loch Broom. U_____
42. Far northern town called Inbhir Ùige in Scots Gaelic. W___

REWARD
You win two red train cards for correctly identifying and finding half of the towns and cities and another two if you can find them all.

FOR SOLUTION SEE PAGE 213

Make Tracks

Rocky beaches without a hint of sand, seagulls swooping on unsuspecting picnickers who leave their food unguarded and multiple windbreaks dotted around to protect from catching a cold; the British seaside holiday is a unique experience. And yet, as soon as the first rays of sun break through the chill, everyone rushes to the beach!

You stand on the new Palace Pier and watch the crowds in amazement. Somehow you are able to resist the impulse to join in, instead making your way to the London and Brighton Railway. The beating heart of the United Kingdom awaits you. You have ten minutes until the next train arrives travelling north, so you turn to your puzzle book to while away the time.

Can you design a railway that connects all of the stations and rail yards before the train arrives? Draw a single continuous line around the grid that passes through every station and rail yard.

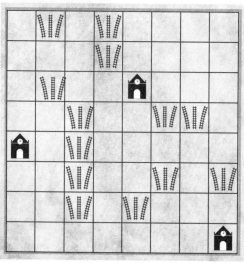

If the line enters a station, turn left or right within its square before passing straight through the next square you come to. Ensure that this works for both routes going in and out of the station.

If the line enters a rail yard, keep going straight through its square before turning left or right in the next square. Ensure that this works for at least one route going into the rail yard.

KEY

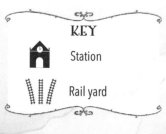

Station

Rail yard

REWARD
If you successfully connect all the stations and yards in 10 minutes, you win two blue train cards. If it takes longer, you win one.

FOR SOLUTION SEE PAGE 213

After Our Swims

Brighton is popular with day trippers from London who travel south in search of fresh air, fun and festivity. Your train carriage is filled with tired families returning home at the end of a long day, sunburned and content. There is still a carnival atmosphere on-board, though, and the hubbub is clearly distracting a bookish young man seated directly opposite you. He eventually abandons his attempts to read, puts down his novel, and engages you in conversation.

He is a clever chap and keen to hear all about your tour so far. He has only been able to "travel" to the Continent himself through his books. The following list of anagrams he shares are all things associated with the British Isles, including the 20th and 21st centuries to come. They all have something in common and there is a clue in the title, which is also an anagram.

Can you unscramble the anagrams and say what binds them together?

1.	UNANCHORED TAYLOR	
2.	LACKED RICHNESS	
3.	MEN FAILING	
4.	GROWL JINK	
5.	LOWER LEG OGRE	
6.	FOOL VIA WIRING	
7.	UNSEAT JEAN	
8.	HAD DOLLAR	
9.	DERAILS COW	
10.	MACHINE BEVY	

A busy
Brighton Beach.

REWARD
If you unscramble all the names, you win two white train cards.

FOR SOLUTION SEE PAGE 214

A Week in London

Few cities can boast as many world-famous landmarks as England's capital. Unfortunately, after spending so much time sampling the delights of continental Europe, and with vast swathes of the world yet to see, you have to restrict your London sightseeing to just one week. Keen to stock up on both experiences and souvenirs, you make a few purchases along the way that you now need to record in your journal.

Can you fill in all the facts from the memories below?

1. You needed a refreshing cup of tea after your long walk into the city; this was the day before you visited Madame Tussaud's wax museum.
2. Your Hackney carriage ride to the Victorian and Albert Museum left you a little queasy and you didn't buy anything to eat or drink for the rest of that day.
3. You didn't buy a map on Wednesday because the newsagent had run out.
4. On the first day of your visit, you had a delicious fish and chip supper. The following morning you visited Trafalgar Square and admired Nelson's Column.
5. Your trip to see Big Ben and the Houses of Parliament inspired you to buy a book about the UK government that you still haven't got round to reading; this wasn't the last day of your visit, and you didn't cycle there.
6. The day you dined on battered cod and fried potatoes wasn't the same day you took the Tube (as the London Underground Railway is known), but the day you rode the Tube was the day before you bought *British Politics for the Clueless*.

Day	Site	Bought	Transport
Monday			
Tuesday			
Wednesday			
Thursday			
Friday			

	V & A Museum	Big Ben	Regent's Park	Madame Tussaud's	Nelson's Column	Flag	Book	Map	Fish and chips	Cup of tea	Walk	Hackney carriage	Bus	Underground	Bicycle
Monday															
Tuesday															
Wednesday															
Thursday															
Friday															
Walk															
Hackney carriage															
Bus															
Underground															
Bicycle															
Flag															
Book															
Map															
Fish and chips															
Cup of tea															

REWARD
If get all the facts, you win three multi-coloured train cards.

FOR SOLUTION SEE PAGE 214

RACE TO THE NORTH

In the 1890s, rival rail companies were unofficially engaged in the so-called "Race to the North" to get their passengers from London to Edinburgh in record time, either by the West Coast Main Line (via Crewe and Carlisle) or the East Coast Main Line (via York and Newcastle). You'd also like to know which is quicker, and upon arrival at London St Pancras ask a passing gentleman and a policeman for their advice. Unfortunately, the policeman says he will only travel on the East line, while the man says that the West has the edge in both speed and comfort.

None the wiser, you leave them to their good-natured bickering and decide to try both trains over a series of days – which has the advantage of both not favouring one line over the other and allowing you to see more sights along the way – before travelling on to begin your Scottish tour.

You must work out the route and insert the tracks into the grid. The numbers on the periphery tell you how many rail sections must be in that row or column, but unnumbered rows and columns may also have rail sections. You may only place a straight or a curved section inside a box. The tracks cannot cross themselves.

Straight

Curve

Can you connect London to Edinburgh?

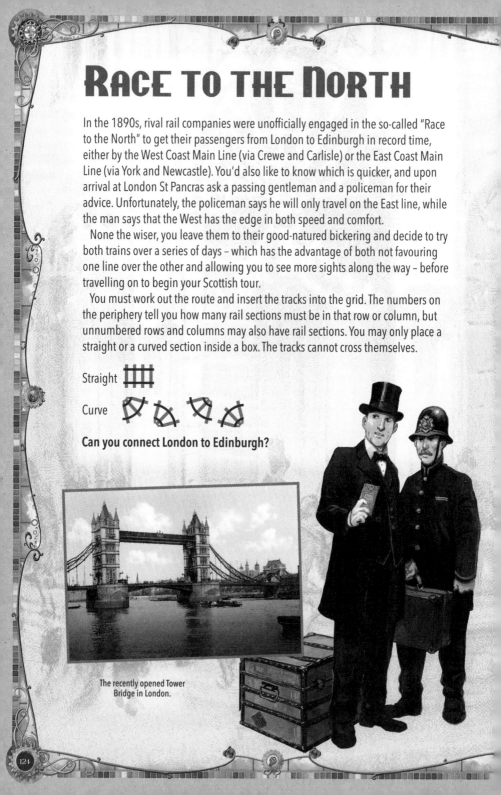

The recently opened Tower Bridge in London.

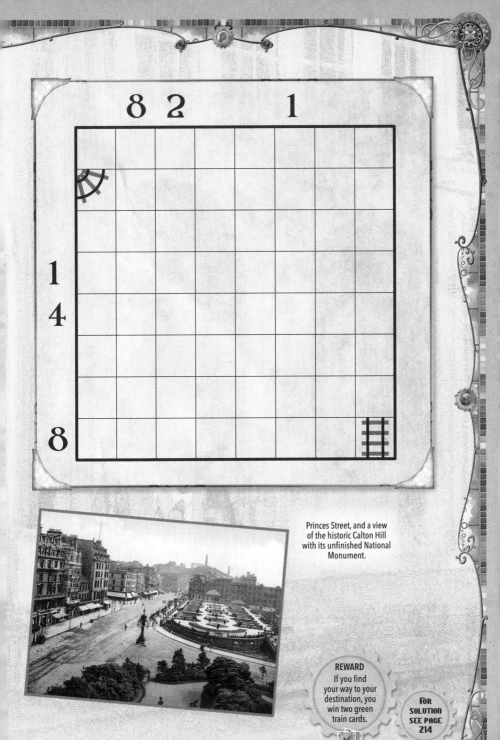

8 2 1

1

4

8

Princes Street, and a view of the historic Calton Hill with its unfinished National Monument.

REWARD
If you find your way to your destination, you win two green train cards.

FOR SOLUTION SEE PAGE 214

Not a Poem

Although it is the birthplace of English, England cannot claim anything like a monopoly on the great writers and orators who employ the language. Your adventure on the island of Ireland brings you to a café in the city of Dublin, overlooking the iconic Ha'penny Bridge, where you meet a mysterious woman who greets you with a curious verse.

"At the end of the sea
the first person to be
angry or crazy
contrived
a fantasy
you hold them in high esteem
but have judged them wrongly –
the merrows!"

O'Connell Bridge in Dublin, with a statue of Daniel O'Donnell visible at the end of it.

DID YOU KNOW?

You can take a steam train from Downpatrick – the burial place of Ireland's patron saint, Patrick – to Inch Abbey, a ruined monastery where *Game of Thrones* was filmed and where the legend of St Patrick banishing the snakes originated.

She's clearly no Oscar Wilde but you politely compliment her on the poem. One thing confuses you. "What are merrows?" you ask.

"It's not a poem, it's a warning!" she intones, while archly furrowing her eyebrows. You are unsurprisingly none the wiser, so you ask for further explanation.

She clarifies that each of the eight lines defines an English word. Each word is made up of the same letters as the one before it (but not necessarily in the same order) plus one more letter. The first word is just a single letter long.

Can you work out the eight words?

REWARD
If you work out what merrows are, you win one black train card

FOR SOLUTION SEE PAGE 214

PAINTING BY NUMBERS

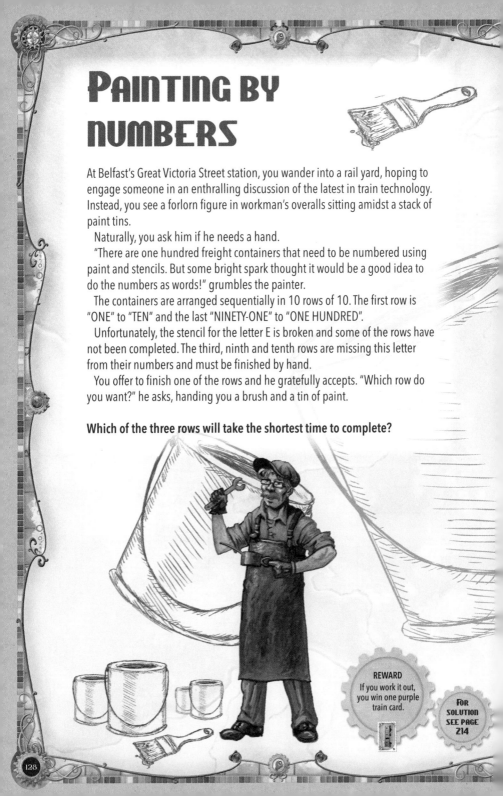

At Belfast's Great Victoria Street station, you wander into a rail yard, hoping to engage someone in an enthralling discussion of the latest in train technology. Instead, you see a forlorn figure in workman's overalls sitting amidst a stack of paint tins.

Naturally, you ask him if he needs a hand.

"There are one hundred freight containers that need to be numbered using paint and stencils. But some bright spark thought it would be a good idea to do the numbers as words!" grumbles the painter.

The containers are arranged sequentially in 10 rows of 10. The first row is "ONE" to "TEN" and the last "NINETY-ONE" to "ONE HUNDRED".

Unfortunately, the stencil for the letter E is broken and some of the rows have not been completed. The third, ninth and tenth rows are missing this letter from their numbers and must be finished by hand.

You offer to finish one of the rows and he gratefully accepts. "Which row do you want?" he asks, handing you a brush and a tin of paint.

Which of the three rows will take the shortest time to complete?

REWARD
If you work it out, you win one purple train card.

FOR SOLUTION SEE PAGE 214

What's Occurin'?

Your next stop takes you to Cardiff. You are amazed to learn that this Welsh town had a population of merely 1,870 people only a century ago. Now there are well over 100,000 inhabitants rushing around you. The dock is so alive with lilting Welsh accents that you grow quite overwhelmed, and decide to duck into the more peaceful environs of the Cardiff Museum.

However, even there you swiftly enter into a lively conversation with the museum director, who tells you of the ongoing efforts to both have Cardiff officially recognized as a city, and for the construction of a dedicated National Museum within the city. It is on your tour that you find a curious document that does not appear to belong to one of the curated collections. You guess that someone in local government had become fed up with bureaucracy and decided to vent their spleen in the form of a puzzle. The page read:

Queen Street, Cardiff, and its new tram system.

On this document the following must be true –

The total number of occurrences of the number 1 is:

The total number of occurrences of the number 2 is:

The total number of occurrences of the number 3 is:

The total number of occurrences of the number 4 is:

The total number of occurrences of the number 5 is:

Can you fill each of the gaps with a single Arabic numeral (the ten digits from 0 to 9) so that the document is true?

REWARD
If you enter the correct numbers, you win 1 yellow train card.

For Solution see page 215

129

Locomotion

Your expedition around the United Kingdom is almost complete. One stormy evening, as you ride a slow train into the rural South East of England, you fall into conversation with a most unusual chap. He astounds you by telling you – from just a brief glance at your attire and luggage – exactly where you are from and which countries you have already been to. Apparently there are telltale signs in the dust that has accumulated on one suitcase, the way that you wear your hat and the pallor of your skin.

As the evening progresses, he entertains you with tales of various fascinating criminal cases that he has solved in the past few years, interspersed with detailed analyses of the origins, professions and characters of various other occupants of your carriage – always unnervingly accurate.

You ask how he came to have such mental acuity, and he smirks, "It's all elementary. But let me set you a little brainteaser that is as good a place to start your training as any."

Ten trains must be placed in the grid opposite. The numbers on the periphery tell you how many squares in that row or column contain a train component (locomotive or carriage). No two trains' components can occupy neighbouring squares (including diagonals).

Can you find…

One train consisting of a locomotive and three carriages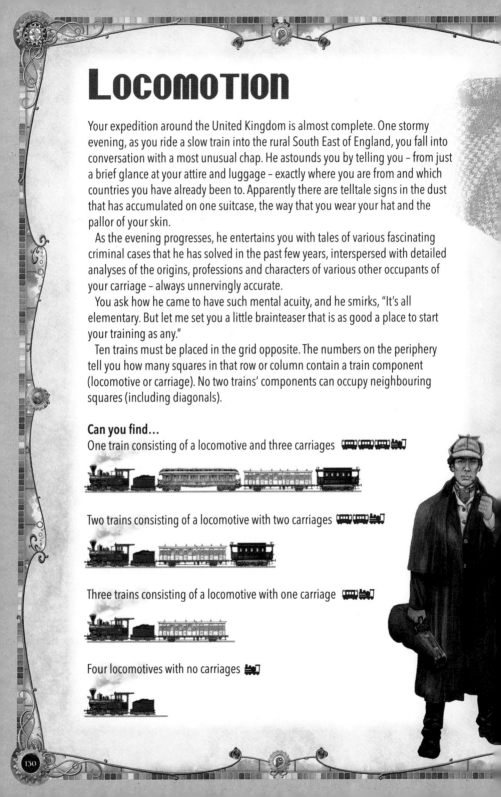

Two trains consisting of a locomotive with two carriages

Three trains consisting of a locomotive with one carriage

Four locomotives with no carriages

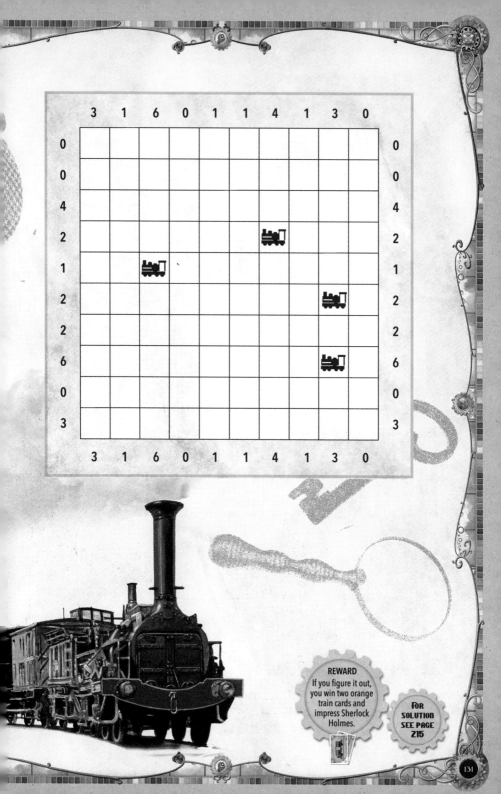

	3	1	6	0	1	1	4	1	3	0	
0											0
0											0
4											4
2							🚂				2
1			🚂								1
2									🚂		2
2											2
6									🚂		6
0											0
3											3
	3	1	6	0	1	1	4	1	3	0	

REWARD
If you figure it out, you win two orange train cards and impress Sherlock Holmes.

FOR SOLUTION SEE PAGE 215

ALL CHANGE!

Your journey around the British Isles has been edifying. The history of each and every town and city you have visited has been fascinating, with many of them able to trace their development back a thousand years or more – and yet the country is at the forefront of modernity, not least with its extensive rail network.

Now you travel north one final time as you prepare to depart from Newcastle and cross the North Sea. Luckily, you have already picked up some thermals in Scotland because the journey is sure to be a cold one.

On the journey, you flick through your keepsakes and pause over two postcards of Piccadilly Circus that you had purchased during your week in London. There appears to be something not quite right about them.

Can you find 12 differences between the picture on the left and the one on the right?

A view of the bustling thoroughfare of Piccadilly Circus.

REWARD
If you find all 12 differences, you win two purple train cards.

FOR SOLUTION SEE PAGE 215

SCANDINAVIA

The far north of Europe is home to a group of countries that have distinctive cultural and linguistic similarities. Natives of Denmark, Sweden, Norway and Iceland speak multiple different North Germanic languages but share an interconnected history from even before the time of the Vikings, while those from Finland and Estonia stand slightly further apart as speaking Uralic languages (distantly related to Hungarian).

The cultural character within this region is largely tied to the natural world: these Nordic countries are known for breathtaking scenery, from icy fjords and endless forests to snow-capped mountain ranges. In the northernmost parts you can experience a summer day without night as well as see the atmospheric phenomenon known as the aurora borealis – the Northern Lights.

Stig ombord!

DISCOVER SCANDINAVIA

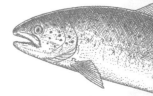

The long sea voyage is over and you arrive at Bergen in the west of Norway, a city that was the largest in Norway until the 1830s. You want to explore the quaint historic port, but if you are honest with yourself what you really want is to find somewhere warm to sit with a hot drink and leave the chill of the North Sea behind you.

The restaurant you choose is bright and friendly. So friendly, in fact, that when the owner learns you are brand-new to the country she insists on serving you some of her delicious fried salmon. Ruefully, you think it would be more delicious if it wasn't paired with your mug of bitter coffee, but you don't mention that to your new friend.

Even better, she agrees to help you plan your trip around Scandinavia. The names of 36 Scandinavian settlements (in a native language) are concealed in the grid opposite. They may run horizontally, vertically, diagonally, forwards or backwards.

To make things more challenging, you must work out which settlements are included by matching them with their facts below.

1.	Main port city on the Limfjord.	Å_____
2.	Terminus of the Rauma Line railway.	Å_____
3.	Denmark's second largest city.	Å_____
4.	Known as the "City of Seven Mountains".	B_____
5.	Originally a rail junction for the Northern and Ore rail lines.	B____
6.	Sweden's second city founded in 1621.	G_____
7.	Host of the 1952 Summer Olympics.	H_____
8.	Mainland Norway's northernmost town.	H_____
9.	Location of Kruununpuisto, Finland's oldest nature reserve.	I_____
10.	Capital of Finland's Kainuu region.	K_____
11.	Location of Sweden's largest naval base.	K_____
12.	Norwegian town closest to Russia.	K_____
13.	Sweden's northernmost town, 40 km from the Esrange Space Center.	K_____
14.	This city is served by the nearby airport often called Kastrup.	K_____
15.	Home of Norway's largest and most popular zoo and amusement park.	K_____
16.	Home of kalakukko – fish baked inside a loaf of bread.	K_____
17.	Once known as the "Chicago of Finland".	L____
18.	Location of the Maihaugen open-air museum.	L_____
19.	Start of the "Blue Highway" international tourist route.	M_ _ _ _
20.	Northern Norwegian ice-free port linked to Sweden by the Iron Ore railway line.	N_____
21.	City by the mouth of the river Motala ström.	N_____
22.	Location of Gustavsvik, one of Scandinavia's largest water parks.	Ö_____
23.	The Nobel Peace Prize is presented here.	O____

Z	N	O	R	R	K	Ö	P	I	N	G	K	V	U	R	W	J	P	H	A	W
G	Ö	L	O	L	L	I	L	L	E	H	A	M	M	E	R	L	S	N	S	W
K	R	S	A	T	I	K	N	I	S	L	E	H	I	B	K	T	O	V	T	O
K	O	O	T	G	U	I	T	H	A	L	P	T	E	Ø	R	R	C	K	A	S
F	L	Q	B	E	M	R	W	X	H	Q	I	R	B	O	K	G	N	U	V	O
H	Z	N	N	L	R	A	K	U	M	I	G	E	M	S	A	Y	M	O	A	H
P	G	F	Q	Å	Å	S	W	U	S	E	N	S	L	A	D	N	Å	P	N	B
E	C	E	T	E	R	W	U	D	N	H	Ø	R	S	A	Z	W	Y	I	G	X
S	Y	E	U	M	F	O	A	N	A	E	A	F	J	P	Y	U	L	O	E	Z
E	Å	R	H	U	S	H	V	V	D	K	F	I	Z	J	I	M	A	T	R	A
N	E	O	I	M	M	L	N	A	K	R	I	S	T	I	A	N	S	A	N	D
E	J	U	N	U	D	O	E	S	N	M	O	L	K	O	P	O	K	N	Ö	K
K	J	V	A	G	L	D	I	X	T	I	I	O	J	X	A	S	M	R	I	L
R	A	S	A	A	V	L	U	R	N	G	E	E	J	N	I	T	E	V	E	L
I	T	Y	J	D	Z	K	G	R	A	S	Ö	M	H	E	S	B	R	T	X	A
K	C	F	A	Q	R	T	O	F	R	N	J	T	I	D	R	A	A	M	U	V
Q	Y	W	K	V	M	T	B	M	P	Q	A	V	E	O	N	M	Y	B	C	S
S	T	O	C	K	H	O	L	M	A	P	I	Z	G	B	P	O	F	K	I	D
S	F	V	L	D	Z	K	I	R	U	N	A	D	Y	E	O	E	R	N	P	N
N	N	I	L	L	A	T	G	E	D	P	R	A	R	V	I	R	H	T	M	U
H	O	N	N	I	N	G	S	V	Å	G	A	E	L	C	P	W	G	U	N	S

24. Known as "Winter City" and the "Centre of Sweden". Ö_____
25. Capital of Lapland. R_____
26. Headquarters of the Norwegian Petroleum Directorate. S_____
27. Most populous city in Scandinavia. S_____
28. After a fire in 1888 it was rebuilt entirely using stone. S_____
29. Home of Vana Toomas ("Old Thomas") the weathervane. T_____
30. The most populous inland city in Scandinavia. T_____
31. Lapland city with dual gauge (Swedish/Finnish) rail tracks. T_____
32. Norway's largest fishing port. T_____
33. Once a capital city known as Nidaros. T_____
34. Former capital of Finland. T_____
35. Known as Björkarnas Stad (the "Town of Birch Trees"). U____
36. Finnish city named after a Swedish royal house. V_____

FOR SOLUTION SEE PAGE 216

Make Tracks

You have heard that a trip on the Bergensbanen to Oslo affords one of the most spectacular scenic train rides in the world, so it is with some excitement that you board the train. You are not disappointed.

The line itself is a marvel of engineering, climbing to 1200 metres high through inhospitable but gloriously beautiful alpine landscapes, affording views of conifer-filled valleys, ice-capped mountains and snowy plateaus along the way. At one remote stop you alight to stretch your legs and make conversation with the guard, who delights in informing you that it took over three decades to build, with more than 180 tunnels having to be carved out of the seemingly impenetrable gneiss of the mountains. He even shares a map showing how they did it.

Can you design a railway that connects all of the stations and rail yards? Draw a single continuous line around the grid that passes through every station and rail yard.

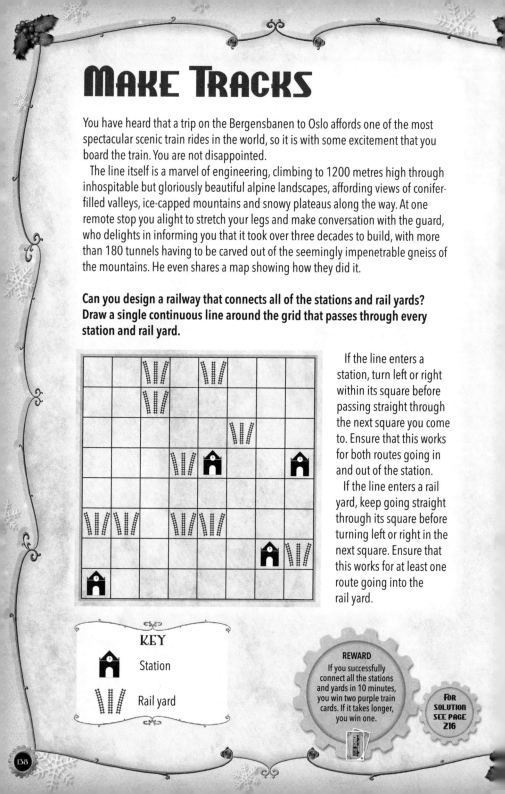

If the line enters a station, turn left or right within its square before passing straight through the next square you come to. Ensure that this works for both routes going in and out of the station.

If the line enters a rail yard, keep going straight through its square before turning left or right in the next square. Ensure that this works for at least one route going into the rail yard.

KEY

Station

Rail yard

REWARD
If you successfully connect all the stations and yards in 10 minutes, you win two purple train cards. If it takes longer, you win one.

FOR SOLUTION SEE PAGE 216

CAST CODE SNARES RATS

The capital of Norway is an attractive city, which makes it all the more of a surprise when you emerge from the station to be greeted by a huge agonised figure screaming against a blood red sky. You blink, and with some relief realise that it is just an oversized poster for an exhibition of Norway's esteemed Expressionist painter Edvard Munch and his collected works, including *The Scream*.

You begin to explore the city, and in particular the Holmenkollbakken, a large ski jumping hill that you make a vow never to try out yourself. However, you can't shake the unease created by the painting, and objects jumble together in your mind.

The following anagrams are people (somehow, all are yet to be born) with a Scandinavian connection. They all have something in common and there is a clue in the title, which is also an anagram.

Can you unscramble the anagrams and say what binds them together to rid yourself of your Munch-inspired anxiety?

1.   **INVALID AIR CAKE**
2.   **MAD ONYX VOWS**
3.   **GRASSLAND STÅLKER**
4.   **SKIMMED ANKLES**
5.   **JAILED ACORNS WALKOUT**
6.   **MACAROON PIE**
7.   **DREAM BRINGING**
8.   **BOGART RAGE**
9.   **BUCCANEERS FORGE**
10. **DRINK BATTLE**

A crowd gathers to watch the experts fly through the air at the Holmenkollbakken.

REWARD
If you unscramble all the names, you win two orange train cards.

FOR SOLUTION SEE PAGE 217

WILDLIFE

The Nordic region is home to many distinctive and striking animals that you are hoping to see running free in their native habitat. Armed with a camera and hiring a local guide in each country, you embark on a long rail journey that takes you deep into the virgin Scandinavian wilderness.

Your tour lasts a full nine months and covers five countries. In each, you saw stunning landscapes and met a number of interesting locals, but memorably in each you had an encounter with a creature that made a lasting impression. Now you must marshal your thoughts and update your journal, recalling when and where you went, with whom you travelled and what you saw.

Can you fill in all the facts from the memories below?

1. In Denmark a guide named Anna accompanied you; this was four months after you saw a musk ox.
2. You travelled to Sweden two months after you accompanied Elizabet into the northern wilderness.
3. Dagmar was your guide during the final month of your tour.
4. Britta showed you the wolverines two months after your trip to Norway.
5. It was in Iceland that you saw the Arctic fox.
6. You did not see any brown bears during the month of August, when you visited Finland.

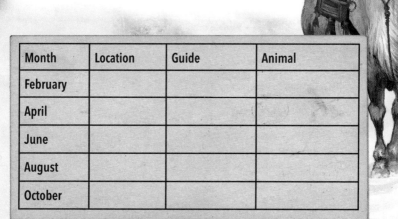

Month	Location	Guide	Animal
February			
April			
June			
August			
October			

	Iceland	Sweden	Denmark	Norway	Finland	Cecilia	Anna	Britta	Elizabet	Dagmar	Musk Ox	Arctic Fox	Eagle	Wolverine	Brown Bear
February															
April															
June															
August															
October															
Musk Ox															
Arctic Fox															
Eagle															
Wolverine															
Brown Bear															
Cecilia															
Anna															
Britta															
Elizabet															
Dagmar															

REWARD
If you get all the facts correct, you win three yellow train cards.

FOR SOLUTION SEE PAGE 217

COPENHAGEN TO GOTHENBURG

While resting for a couple of days in Copenhagen during your wilderness wanderings, you receive a telegram from Britta, your Swedish friend, telling you that she has heard rumours of a wild wolf sighting nearby. She lives around Gothenburg, and plans to set off on an expedition to track them the very next day.

   This is "AN OPPORTUNITY THAT CANNOT BE MISSED" – as her telegram shouts at you – because the wolf was hunted to near extinction in Sweden mere decades ago. You hastily check out of your hotel and rush to the station. The problem is that there is no easy way to cross the Sound between Denmark and Sweden. You must figure out the best route to get to Gothenburg, but you only have five minutes to do it!

   Can you work out the route and insert the tracks into the grid below within the time limit? The numbers on the periphery tell you how many rail sections must be in that row or column. You may place only a straight or a curved section inside a box. The tracks cannot cross themselves.

Straight

Curve

Can you connect Copenhagen to Gothenburg?

The Tivoli Gardens amusement park in Copenhagen. Not much wildlife on show there.

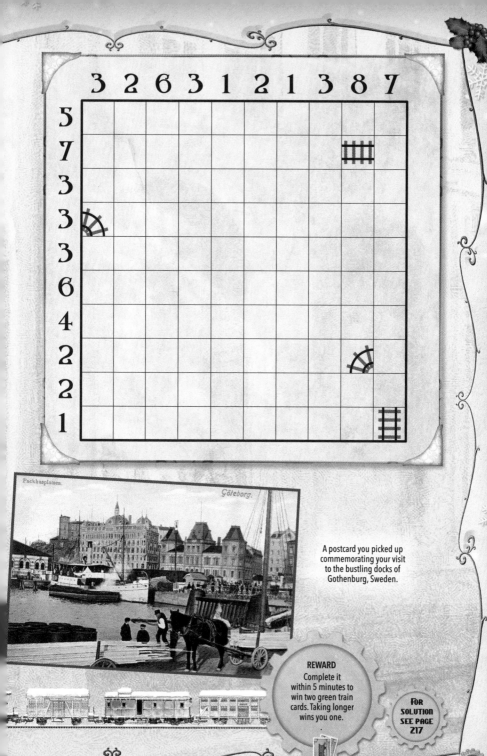

A postcard you picked up commemorating your visit to the bustling docks of Gothenburg, Sweden.

REWARD
Complete it within 5 minutes to win two green train cards. Taking longer wins you one.

FOR SOLUTION SEE PAGE 217

FLAGS

Despite their Viking legacies, the Nordic countries are noted for their progressive and peaceful outlooks, and they are generally recognized as some of the happiest places on Earth. You have certainly felt cheerful since almost the first moment you arrived (excepting the salmon and coffee combination of the first evening).

You remark upon this to your friend Anna. "It is true," she says with a smile, "that we are content. Why shouldn't we be? We have beautiful countryside, good food and long summer evenings to enjoy. And it helps when you like your neighbours, too."

She tells you of shifting national borders and good-natured rivalries that have resulted in some curious hangovers, such as the southern Swedish region of Skåne. There, the population has strong links to Denmark, and the local flag and dialect are more than a little Danish!

Can you divide the grid opposite into four regions of the same shape, made up of an equal number of squares, each containing a representation of each of the four flags?

Norway

Denmark

Sweden

Finland

		SE			FI
	DK		SE	DK	
		FI	NO		
NO		FI	FI		
SE	DK	SE	NO		
NO					DK

REWARD
If you divide the grid correctly, you win 1 blue train card.

FOR SOLUTION SEE PAGE 217

Nature Trail

A train takes you from Helsinki to Kolari in Finnish Lapland. Your ultimate destination is the Pallastunturi Fells, which lies in the midst of more than 1,000 square kilometres of fells and taiga forests.

You have signed up for an organised nature trail led by a man who appears as if he has lived in these snowy climes for decades, and with a sense of mischief to match. He has set up a route to the falls that requires you to visit 19 waypoints before making camp at grid location A3 on the map opposite. The distance between each square on the grid is 1 kilometre, and at each waypoint you must follow his instructions, given inside the square on the grid, to reach the next. The camp itself counts as a waypoint.

What are your starting coordinates?

	A	B	C	D	
1	1km South	1km East	2km South	3km West	1
2	1km East	3km South	1km East	1km North	2
3	CAMP	2km North	1km North	2km South	3
4	1km South	2km East	2km West	1km North	4
5	2km North	1km North	1km North	1km West	5
	A	B	C	D	

REWARD
If you successfully reach the camp, you win one multi-coloured train card.

FOR SOLUTION SEE PAGE 218

MIDSUMMER

The Summer solstice is a time of jubilation in the Nordic countries. In Sweden the longest day is celebrated as a national holiday, a time for family and friends to get together to sing, dance, eat and drink.

Your friend Erik has invited you to a Midsummer party. Tables and chairs have been arranged out in the open air and the guests are chatting happily to one another while they wait for the first course to be served. All except one…

"Who's the fellow sitting alone over there?"

You nod to a red-faced man, who seems to be grumbling something to himself about the children having too much fun, the food being too dry and, bizarrely, the sun shining excessively. He does not seem too concerned that the chairs opposite and beside him are empty.

"Oh, that's 'Uncle Carl'," replies your host with a laugh and a shake of his head. "Every year he comes and complains about everything and everyone at the party. I'm sure he enjoys it, but it can get quite tiring… so this year I came up with a solution."

"You're going to make him sit alone?"

"That would be rude. I reserved the four seats at his table for my father's brother-in-law, my brother's father-in-law, my father-in-law's brother and my brother-in-law's father."

"So, the other three haven't arrived yet?" you ask.

"Oh yes, they have," replies your host with a wicked grin, "they're all at their correct table."

Can you demonstrate how Erik's cunning plan works?

You took part in the dance around the maypole, a typical celebration of Midsummer in Sweden.

REWARD
If you figure it out, you win one red train card.

FOR SOLUTION SEE PAGE 218

PASSAGE OF TIME

You travel to Sápmi in the northernmost region of Scandinavia, which is the home of the Sámi people and is sometimes referred to as Lapland.

It is the middle of winter and festivities are currently underway. Your unerring ability to make friends has earned you an invitation to a party on the outskirts of Jokkmokk. After locating the sturdy timber meeting hall, stamping the snow from your boots and shedding many layers of thermal clothing, you gratefully accept a hot mug of coffee from a woman who looks older than the mountains.

She introduces herself as "Akka", which also happens to be the name of the Sámi, Finnish and Estonian Mother Goddess and means "old lady".

Akka is well aware that her age is a source of curiosity and laughs when her granddaughter asks you to guess how many winters she has seen. You attempt to be diplomatic, but she waves your stammerings away.

"Two days ago, she was a mere 97 years old," chuckles her granddaughter, "but next year she will be 100!"

You look at Akka, who nods solemnly. Is Akka pulling your leg?

REWARD
If you figure it out, you win one white train card.

FOR SOLUTION SEE PAGE Z18

ALL CHANGE!

You have spent more than a year travelling northern Europe, and have experienced both the ethereal enchantment of the Northern Lights and the strangely disorientating everlasting day, when the sun never sets, even in the dead of "night". It is a land like no other you have come across, and it is with a heavy heart that you decide it is time to move on.

Before you leave for good, you return to Bergen, where your journey began. The smells draw you back to the fish market – where you sample some of the freshest catch you will ever have the opportunity to eat – and which you learn has been in operation since the 12th century. Speaking of 12...

Can you find 12 differences between the picture on the left and the one on the right?

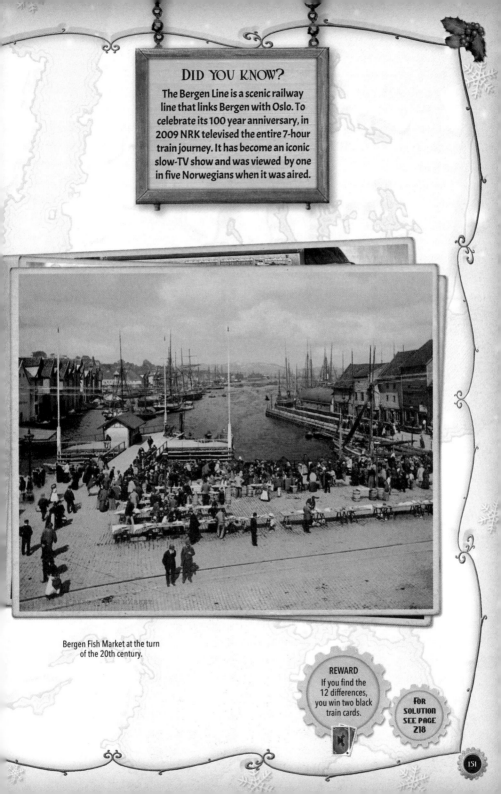

DID YOU KNOW?

The Bergen Line is a scenic railway line that links Bergen with Oslo. To celebrate its 100 year anniversary, in 2009 NRK televised the entire 7-hour train journey. It has become an iconic slow-TV show and was viewed by one in five Norwegians when it was aired.

Bergen Fish Market at the turn of the 20th century.

REWARD
If you find the 12 differences, you win two black train cards.

FOR SOLUTION SEE PAGE 218

Asia

The world's largest continent, Asia stretches from its eastern shores on the Pacific Ocean to the borders of both Europe and Africa in the west, the Arctic in the north and the Indian Ocean in the south.

Asia is the birthplace of some of humanity's earliest civilizations and is home to the majority of the world's human beings. China and India are among the Asian nations that have contributed to the continent's remarkable cultural progress and economic prosperity throughout the centuries.

Unsurprisingly, Asia also hosts much of the world's longest train journey: the Trans-Siberian Railway route, which would eventually stretch from Moscow to Vladivostok over a breathtaking 9,289km!

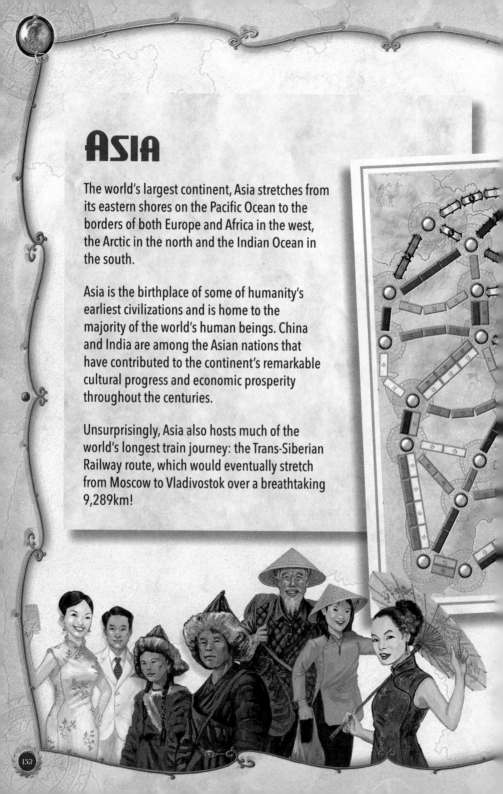

DISCOVER ASIA

Entering a new continent is always an adventure and you decide to throw yourself in at the deep end by travelling straight to one of the busiest cities in the world, currently called Bombay. You disembark at the world famous Victoria Terminus and are immediately hit by a wall of heat, sound and smell that is as exhilarating as it is disorientating after the cool, calm train interior.

After refuelling on some delightful street food you decide to find somewhere to sit to regain your bearings… and to give your mouth a chance to cool off. You will quickly have to get used to the strong spices that flavour every meal – from breakfast to dinner – in this corner of the world!

The names of 38 cities from Asia and transcontinental Russia are hidden in the grid opposite. They may run horizontally, vertically, diagonally, forwards or backwards.

Note that many of the names are westernized (predominantly English) versions dating back to the end of the 19th century, although some of the clues refer to places and events from later on.

To make things more challenging, you must work out which cities are included by matching them with their facts below.

1.   The city where you can find the Taj Mahal.   A____
2.   Replaced Constantinople as its nation's capital.   A_____
3.   City on the Volga, formerly known as Xacitarxan/Hajji Tarkhan.   A_____
4.   Its full name is the world's longest place name.   B_____
5.   Location of an historic rail terminus, now known as Chhatrapati Shivaji.   B_____
6.   Capital of West Bengal.   C_____
7.   Joined the Trans-Siberian Railway in 1900.   C____
8.   Commercial capital of Ceylon (now Sri Lanka).   C_____
9.   Capital of Xinjiang.   D____
10. Location of the Ho Chi Minh Mausoleum.   H____
11. This city's flag features a tiger with a sable in its mouth.   I____
12. Pakistan's "City of Lights".   K_____
13. Capital of Nepal.   K_____
14. Major Russian city 30km from the Chinese border.   K_____
15. Capital of Japan's Hyōgo Prefecture.   K____
16. The Siberian Federal University was founded here in 2006.   K_____
17. Capital of Tibet.   L____
18. Former Portuguese colony transferred to China in 1999.   M___
19. Home of "the world's largest book", the Tripitaka stone tablets.   M___
20. Islam's holiest city.   M___
21. Home of Saint Basil's Cathedral and the Bolshoi theatre.   M___
22. City located on the junction of the Om and Irtysh rivers.   O____
23. Location of the vast palace complex known as the Forbidden City.   P____
24. A major rail hub known as Molotov between 1940 and 1957.   P____
25. Capital of Burma (Myanmar) until 2005.   R____
26. City intertwined with neighbouring Islamabad.   R_____

K	O	T	S	O	V	I	D	A	L	V	O	D	G	B	D	K	A	J	M	V
X	K	C	S	P	T	D	Y	Y	T	M	M	N	S	H	A	N	G	H	A	I
S	T	Z	J	T	A	I	P	E	I	N	I	U	C	W	C	L	V	Z	X	Q
A	Y	A	B	M	O	B	Y	A	A	K	Y	K	R	J	C	D	C	D	N	S
M	O	S	C	O	W	D	J	R	E	C	O	A	T	C	E	I	Q	T	I	P
A	I	G	D	L	O	Y	H	P	G	P	H	B	L	X	M	H	I	N	B	K
R	D	K	D	P	S	E	H	T	E	K	I	I	K	A	I	U	G	Z	S	Q
K	N	O	Y	W	T	S	G	C	K	L	S	K	T	P	D	A	D	V	X	S
A	I	K	W	P	E	Z	A	R	I	H	S	R	K	A	P	N	O	I	K	U
N	P	G	Y	E	D	J	O	S	A	C	I	S	A	O	G	R	A	A	S	G
D	L	N	M	R	D	T	I	N	O	H	T	G	R	Y	A	N	T	M	M	W
T	A	A	W	M	A	H	O	L	C	U	A	E	H	B	O	H	K	O	B	E
C	W	B	Z	B	Y	I	O	A	K	Y	D	T	A	M	M	N	V	A	Q	M
A	A	J	N	N	L	M	R	R	O	B	T	H	S	A	M	X	S	J	M	A
L	R	A	C	N	B	A	I	O	O	N	K	K	N	L	P	T	M	A	N	R
C	L	I	I	O	K	J	D	A	A	W	A	D	H	H	R	S	A	N	R	A
U	K	R	D	O	Q	V	N	R	F	B	U	A	D	A	U	A	C	X	S	K
T	U	A	W	G	N	M	E	M	X	A	J	X	K	S	T	I	A	I	E	N
T	R	F	Z	N	L	Y	J	Z	G	B	F	H	J	A	H	G	U	B	O	A
A	I	T	F	A	N	P	U	R	Y	K	A	P	E	B	K	O	T	V	U	M
O	G	O	E	R	X	H	A	N	Y	N	N	Z	A	I	W	N	B	G	L	V

27. Its name changed to Ho Chi Minh City in 1976.   S_____
28. Original capital of the Timurid Empire.   S_____
29. Location of the Changdeokgung Palace.   S____
30. Host of the Chinese Grand Prix since 2004.   S_____
31. The tomb of the Persian poet Hafez can be found here.   S_____
32. City-state off the southern tip of the Malay Peninsula.   S_____
33. Capital of the Republic of China (Taiwan).   T_____
34. Capital of Georgia.   T_____
35. Agha Mohammad Khan Qajar made it a capital.   T_____
36. Mongolia's largest city.   U___ _____
37. Russia's largest Pacific port.   V_____
38. The Terracotta Army was discovered outside this city.   X___

REWARD

You win two green train cards for correctly identifying and finding half of all of the cities and another two if you can find them all.

FOR SOLUTION SEE PAGE 219

Make Tracks

India is a diverse and bustling country. From the street food (your tolerance of spice has thankfully increased!) and kids playing cricket on the dirt roads, to the wondrous Taj Mahal in Agra and the Red Fort in Delhi, it offers everything from spectacular high culture to everyday delights. What's more, the railway is modern and efficient, and so you decide to take a whistle-stop tour right around the country.

However, the railway lines seem to criss-cross haphazardly and you are struggling to figure out the most efficient route that stops at all of the major cities and landmarks.

Can you design a route that connects all of the cities and landmarks?
Draw a single continuous line around the grid that passes through every city and landmark.

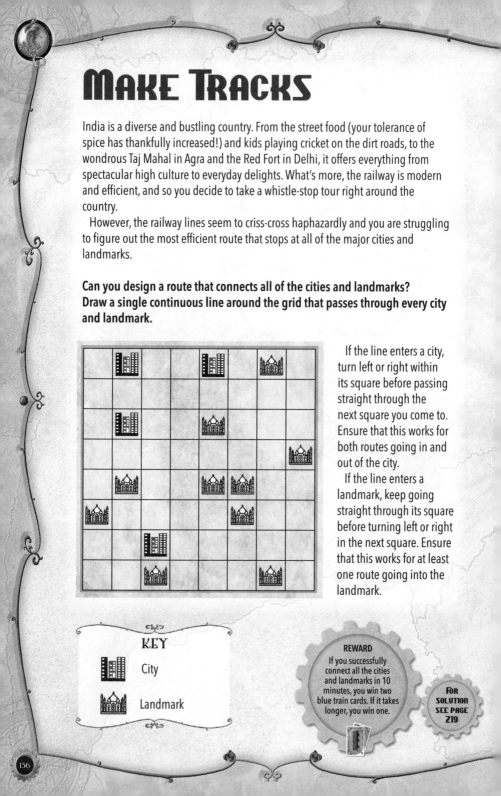

If the line enters a city, turn left or right within its square before passing straight through the next square you come to. Ensure that this works for both routes going in and out of the city.

If the line enters a landmark, keep going straight through its square before turning left or right in the next square. Ensure that this works for at least one route going into the landmark.

FOR SOLUTION SEE PAGE 219

KEY

City

Landmark

REWARD
If you successfully connect all the cities and landmarks in 10 minutes, you win two blue train cards. If it takes longer, you win one.

A Jar Spawned No Sole

India is vast, but it is only when you begin to look east that the true scale of Asia hits you. You spend long days chugging through an ever-changing continent, alighting at rural stations to make friends and learn something of the customs and cultures of the people you meet.

It is on one of these brief visits that you meet a fascinating character. Despite the language barrier, she warms to you immediately and happily takes you around her village, pointing to various objects and trying to teach you about them. In amongst the somewhat bewildering stream of language, you catch the occasional word that sounds familiar to you, but everything is a bit of a jumble.

The following anagrams are things with an Asian connection that the woman may have talked about, although some come from later in time. They all have something in common and there is a clue in the title, which is also an anagram.

Can you unscramble the anagrams and say what binds them together?

1.   I MEAN
2.   FOUNT
3.   OAK RAKE
4.   A TAKER
5.   I AM GIRO
6.   ASIA RUM
7.   HAS SUIT
8.   AIRY KITE
9.   NUTS AIM

REWARD
If you unscramble all the words, you win two orange train cards.

FOR SOLUTION SEE PAGE 220

TAKE YOUR SEAT

In the far north of Asia you make a journey on the recently completed Trans-Siberian Railway, the incredible engineering feat that runs nearly 10,000km from Moscow to Vladivostok.

Excitedly, you board a carriage with seven other passengers, each of you well wrapped up against the cold and looking forward to a warming drink and the start of your journey.

The carriage consists of eight rows of seats, and you decide that in order to maximise your sightseeing opportunities, each of the passengers will take a seat on a different row. Writing later in your journal, you try to recall where you sat. Here are some clues:

You did not take the seat closest to the engine, but you were closer to it than Boris.

Boris had a seat that was further from the engine than Yelena, who was further away from it than Tatiana, who was further than Nikita, who was one seat closer to it than Victor.

Sofia was further from the engine than Boris and twice as far from it as Tatiana. Yelena was twice as far from the engine as Oleg.

Can you work out which seat you took?

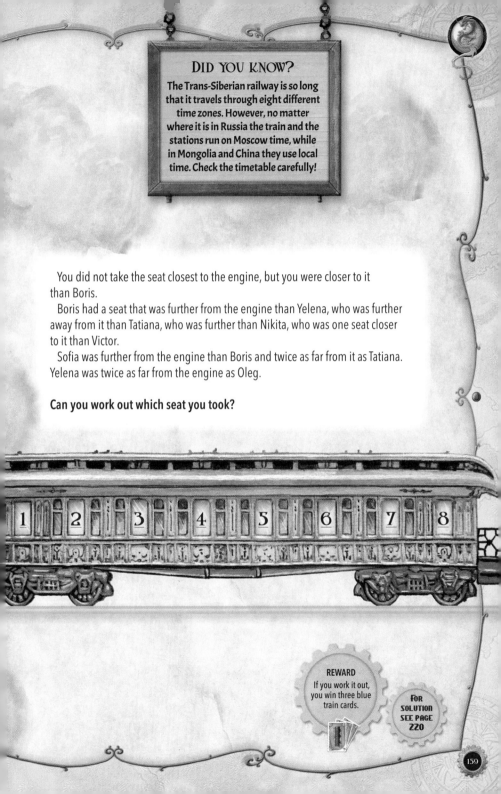

FOR SOLUTION SEE PAGE 220

TRANS-SIBERIA

Although the Trans-Siberian Railway opened in 1904, works are still ongoing to expand its reach. As you continue your multiple-day journey, you fall in with the crew and have a number of late night discussions over hot cups of sbiten about their adventures and what cities these new lines will allow them to explore.

From their thoughts, you create a map of sorts in your journal showing the route from Moscow to Vladivostok. Can you work out the route and insert the tracks into the grid opposite?

The numbers on the periphery tell you how many rail sections must be in that row or column.

You may place only a straight or a curved section inside a box. The tracks cannot cross themselves.

Straight

Curve

Can you connect Moscow to Vladivostok?

You couldn't get inside the Kremlin to explore, but did get to appreciate the view.

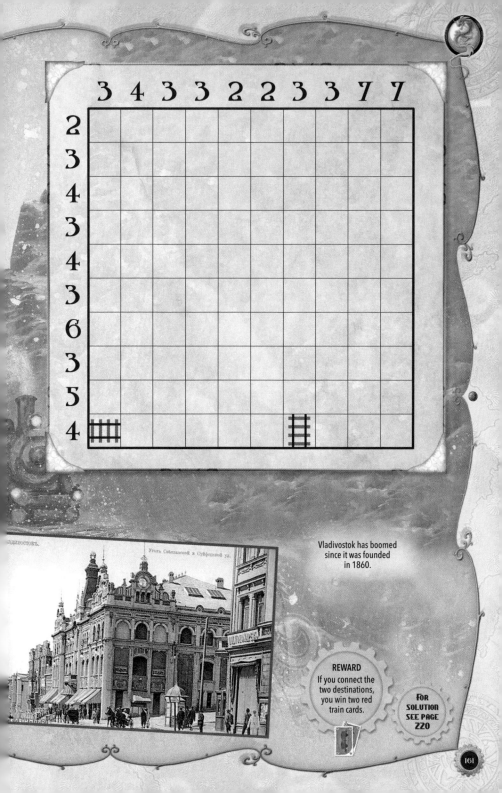

Vladivostok has boomed since it was founded in 1860.

REWARD
If you connect the two destinations, you win two red train cards.

FOR SOLUTION SEE PAGE 220

ARABIC NUMERALS

Having already travelled around almost half the world, you are becoming something of a dab hand at helping railway employees with their conundrums. So, when you are preparing to take the partially-constructed Hejaz railway (that will soon travel from Damascus down to Medina), and find a forlorn worker scratching his head, you waste no time to ask if he needs assistance.

He points at the two trains that are standing on opposite platforms, each consisting of an engine and four carriages. You notice that the carriages are colour coded and that each has a single numeral made of cast iron fixed to it. The worker has evidently just finished screwing these numbers onto the carriages.

He tells you: "My supervisor gave me two sets of numbers and told me to attach them so that the red carriages have the lowest values and the blue carriages the highest. He said that when I add the numbers of each train's carriages together, both trains should have the same total. But that one comes to 19 and the other to 20. I'm sure I've mixed up one of the pairs!"

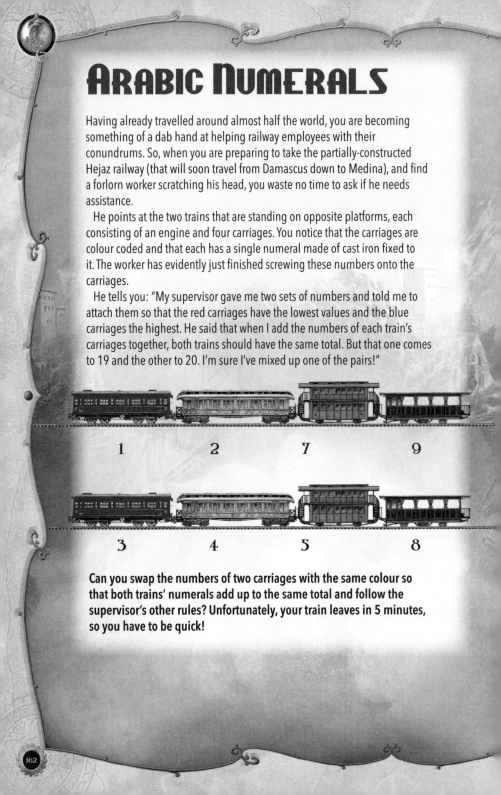

1   2   7   9

3   4   5   8

Can you swap the numbers of two carriages with the same colour so that both trains' numerals add up to the same total and follow the supervisor's other rules? Unfortunately, your train leaves in 5 minutes, so you have to be quick!

DID YOU KNOW?

Work started on the Hejaz railway in 1900 and it opened in 1908 as a key route for pilgrims. However, just a decade later the route was abandoned after the track was damaged. Many of the stations are preserved as museums, along with the original locomotives.

最飞的行月五
蔵快玩
旅途愉快

REWARD
If you figure it out, you win one black train card. If it takes you less than five minutes, you win two.

FOR SOLUTION SEE PAGE 220

A Dream of Things to Come

You are back in East Asia, and your train journey across Japan is tranquil this time. Cherry trees blossom outside the window of your carriage like an endless pink sea, lulling you to sleep and into a curious dream…

You are transported to a future time where the super-fast Tokaido Shinkansen connects Tokyo to Osaka, a 515km rail journey completed in just two-and-a-half hours! Surely that will never be possible, but in the world of sleep, anything can happen.

To your delight, you discover that the passengers of this futuristic era keep their minds active with a new kind of puzzle. Your subconscious is determined to solve one before you awake!

Can you fill in the grid below so that each row, each column and each of the nine 3x3 boxes contains the numbers 1 to 9?

		3					6	1
8				4				
			8					2
					6			5
			1			3	9	
			2	9				
9		5		2			7	
				8			2	3
	4					5		

REWARD
If you solve the sudoku, you win one yellow train card. If you complete it in less than 10 minutes, you win two.

FOR SOLUTION SEE PAGE 220

TECHNOLOGY

In Shanghai you observe four mysterious crates being loaded onto a freight train, evidently bound for Europe. Curious, you strike up a conversation with a fellow world traveller and his daughter, who appear to be the owners of the freight, and are only too delighted to chat with you.

"I'm not supposed to reveal the contents," he says, "but my daughter could give you some clues."

"The more cryptic the better!" you reply enthusiastically.

"Well, there are four different devices…
One uses thousands of near-identical components.
Two of them require potential energy to function.
One has three obvious moving parts and is portable.
Three of them have no mechanical components at all.
One cannot work without a specific type of radiation.
One requires a constant flow of electrons.
All four devices fulfil the same function."

What could the devices be?

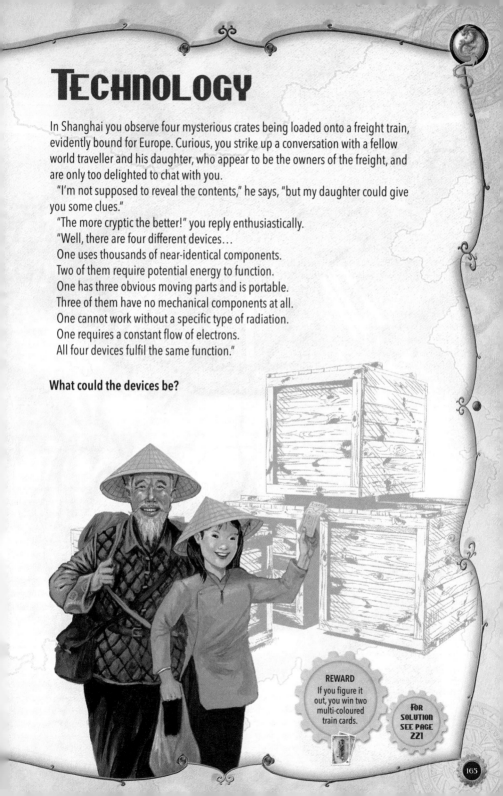

REWARD
If you figure it out, you win two multi-coloured train cards.

FOR SOLUTION SEE PAGE 221

LOCOMOTION

For your final journey, you travel through Bangkok, Saigon and Singapore to the farthest southern reaches of Asia. On the way, you fall in with a young woman and when you discover that she too is a lover of railways, you quickly become firm friends.

She is not just great company and an intelligent tour guide around the many impressive Buddhist temples that you visit, but she also shares another passion of yours – puzzles! While you are waiting outside one particular station, she sets you a challenge.

Ten trains must be placed in the grid opposite. The numbers on the periphery tell you how many squares in that row or column contain a train component (locomotive or carriage). No two trains' components can occupy neighbouring squares (including diagonals).

Can you find…

One train consisting of a locomotive and three carriages

Two trains consisting of a locomotive with two carriages

Three trains consisting of a locomotive with one carriage

Four locomotives with no carriages

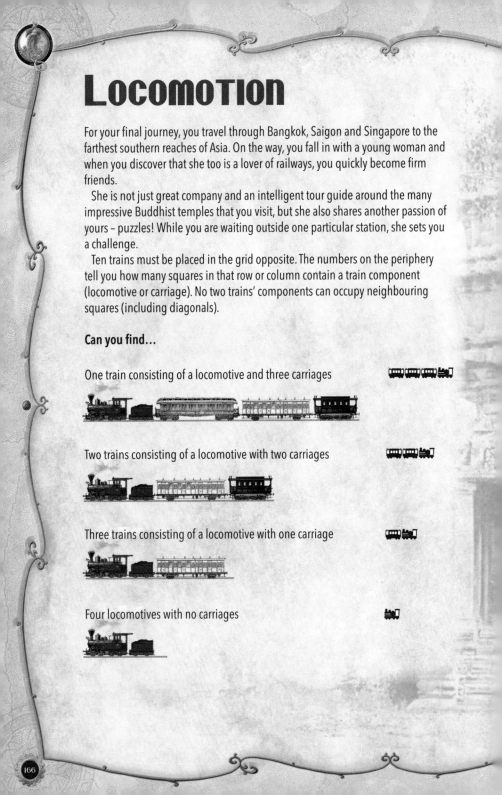

	0	4	1	3	1	4	1	4	2	0	
6											6
2											2
2											2
2											2
0											0
2											2
0											0
6											6
0											0
0											0
	0	4	1	3	1	4	1	4	2	0	

The Angkor Wat temple complex is the largest religious structure in the world by land area.

REWARD
If you figure it out, you win two purple train cards.

FOR SOLUTION SEE PAGE 221

ALL CHANGE!

Sadly, your Asian adventure is coming to a close. Although you have spent months roaming the continent, you feel as if you have only just scratched the surface of it, and you hope that you will get the chance to return at some point in the future. You have also decided that your next leg will be something a little different.

Rather than confine yourself to just one country or continent, you decide that your travelling skills are ready to take on the whole world! There will be just as many sails as rails in your near future. Before you leave Japan, though, you decide to try out your painting skills and make a copy of a postcard you just picked up. You create a near-perfect copy, with just a few small mistakes.

Can you find the 12 differences between the picture on the left and the one on the right?

DID YOU KNOW?

It is believed that the first person to reach the summit of Mount Fuji was a monk in the 7th century. Now this active volcano is one of the most climbed mountains in the world, with more than 200,000 people ascending it each year.

Mount Fuji as seen from Fujinomiya in Shizuoka Prefecture.

REWARD
If you find all 12 differences, you win two yellow train cards.

FOR SOLUTION SEE PAGE 221

Rails & Sails

The final part of your journey will take you around the world by land and sea. Global travel is a rare privilege, and while you aren't quite Ferdinand Magellan, you still feel the thrill of setting off into the unknown as your first ship sets sail.

Early civilizations such as the Greeks, Romans and Han Chinese travelled to expand their territories across continents and coastal waters, but it was seafarers – like the Vikings and Polynesians, among others – who first dared to journey across uncharted seas to find new lands.

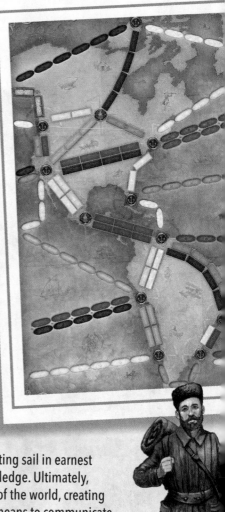

By the early fifteenth century, during the so-called Age of Discovery, European explorers were setting sail in earnest with dreams of exotic wealth and knowledge. Ultimately, trade routes would link the continents of the world, creating diplomatic ties or at the very least the means to communicate across the globe.

Although the world today is well mapped and documented, there still remains much for an aspiring explorer to discover!

DISCOVER THE WORLD

Your time at sea passes smoothly, but the unchanging landscape – the vast, vast ocean – does not afford nearly as many sightseeing opportunities as you are used to on your rail travels. Fortunately, your amiable personality and the long days on board give you the chance to make lifelong friends.

You discover that one of these new friends, a woman who took the cabin next to yours when you left Japan, is a young anthropologist who has already visited every continent the world has to offer (which is secretly your goal as well). She is only too happy to share her knowledge of the world to help you plan your next steps.

The names of 42 world locations are concealed in the grid opposite. They may run horizontally, vertically, diagonally, forwards or backwards.

To make things more challenging, you must work out which locations are included by matching them with their facts below.

1.	Known as the "City of a Thousand Minarets".	A_-Q_____
2.	Alaska's largest city, founded as a camp town for Alaska Railroad in 1914.	A_____
3.	The Hellenic Parliament assembles at this city's Old Royal Palace.	A_____
4.	Location of the Buddhist temples Wat Arun and Wat Pho.	B_____
5.	The world's most populous capital.	B_____
6.	Capital located on the western shore of the Río de la Plata.	B_____ A____
7.	Largest settlement on Canada's Victoria Island.	C_____ ___
8.	South Africa's "Mother City".	C___ ____
9.	Venezuelan city where Simón Bolivar was born.	C_____
10.	Morocco's chief port and largest city.	C_____
11.	Became New Zealand's first official city in 1856.	C_____
12.	This city's name means "Place of Peace" in Arabic.	D__ __ ____
13.	Capital of Australia's Northern Territory.	D_____
14.	Now known as the "Pearl of the Gulf of Tadjoura".	D_____
15.	Lothian city called Dùn Èideann in Scots Gaelic.	E_____
16.	Location of the Speicherstadt (City of Warehouses).	H_____
17.	Special Administrative Region transferred to China in 1997.	H___ ____
18.	State capital located on the island of Oahu.	H_____
19.	Flood-prone city on the north-west coast of Java.	J_____
20.	Capital of Nigeria until 1991.	L____
21.	Capital of Pakistan's Punjab region.	L_____
22.	Peruvian and ex-Incan city known as City of the Kings.	L__
23.	Location of the Griffith Observatory.	L__ _____
24.	Angola's primary port city founded in 1576.	L_____
25.	Home to Binondo, the world's oldest Chinatown.	M_____
26.	France's oldest city.	M_____
27.	Florida's "Magic City".	M____
28.	Birthplace of Wassily Kandinsky and Fyodor Dostoevsky.	M_____
29.	Home of Bollywood (Hindi cinema).	M_____
30.	Location of Central Park and Times Square.	N__ ____

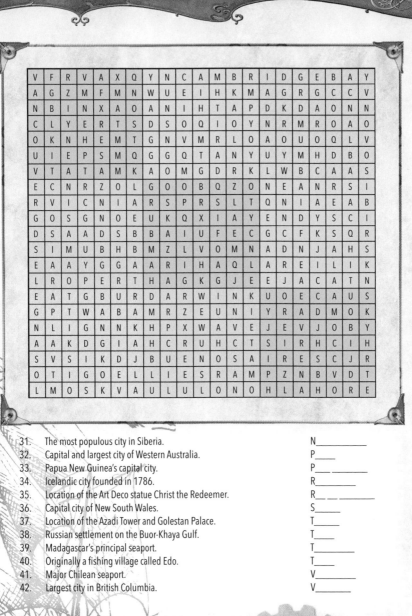

V	F	R	V	A	X	Q	Y	N	C	A	M	B	R	I	D	G	E	B	A	Y
A	G	Z	M	F	M	N	W	U	E	I	H	K	M	A	G	R	G	C	C	V
N	B	I	N	X	A	O	A	N	I	H	T	A	P	D	K	D	A	O	N	N
C	L	Y	E	R	T	S	D	S	O	Q	I	O	Y	N	R	M	R	O	A	O
O	K	N	H	E	M	T	G	N	V	M	R	L	O	A	O	U	O	Q	L	V
U	I	E	P	S	M	Q	G	G	Q	T	A	N	Y	U	Y	M	H	D	B	O
V	T	A	T	A	M	K	A	O	M	G	D	R	K	L	W	B	C	A	A	S
E	C	N	R	Z	O	L	G	O	O	B	Q	Z	O	N	E	A	N	R	S	I
R	V	I	C	N	I	A	R	S	P	R	S	L	T	Q	N	I	A	E	A	B
G	O	S	G	N	O	E	U	K	Q	X	I	A	Y	E	N	D	Y	S	C	I
D	S	A	A	D	S	B	B	A	I	U	F	E	C	G	C	F	K	S	Q	R
S	I	M	U	B	H	B	M	Z	L	V	O	M	N	A	D	N	J	A	H	S
E	A	A	Y	G	G	A	A	R	I	H	A	Q	L	A	R	E	I	L	I	K
L	R	O	P	E	R	T	H	A	G	K	G	J	E	E	J	A	C	A	T	N
E	A	T	G	B	U	R	D	A	R	W	I	N	K	U	O	E	C	A	U	S
G	P	T	W	A	B	A	M	R	Z	E	U	N	I	Y	R	A	D	M	O	K
N	L	I	G	N	N	K	H	P	X	W	A	V	E	J	E	V	J	O	B	Y
A	A	K	D	G	I	A	H	C	R	U	H	C	T	S	I	R	H	C	I	H
S	V	S	I	K	D	J	B	U	E	N	O	S	A	I	R	E	S	C	J	R
O	T	I	G	O	E	L	L	I	E	S	R	A	M	P	Z	N	B	V	D	T
L	M	O	S	K	V	A	U	L	U	L	O	N	O	H	L	A	H	O	R	E

31. The most populous city in Siberia.   N_____
32. Capital and largest city of Western Australia.   P_____
33. Papua New Guinea's capital city.   P___ _____
34. Icelandic city founded in 1786.   R_____
35. Location of the Art Deco statue Christ the Redeemer.   R__ __ _____
36. Capital city of New South Wales.   S_____
37. Location of the Azadi Tower and Golestan Palace.   T_____
38. Russian settlement on the Buor-Khaya Gulf.   T____
39. Madagascar's principal seaport.   T_____
40. Originally a fishing village called Edo.   T____
41. Major Chilean seaport.   V_____
42. Largest city in British Columbia.   V_____

REWARD
You win two red train cards for correctly identifying and finding half of all of the cities and another two if you can find them all.

FOR SOLUTION SEE PAGE 222

Make Tracks

The route you decide on is a complex one, made all the more so by the fact that you now have to navigate by both land and sea. It's a good thing, then, that apart from one thrilling morning when whales were sighted off the prow of the ship, there is little else to do on board but make plans and dream of your future travels.

Can you design a journey that connects all of the train stations and ports? Draw a single continuous line around the grid that passes through every train station and port.

   If the line enters a train station, turn left or right within its square before passing straight through the next square you come to. Ensure that this works for both routes going in and out of the train station.
   If the line enters a port, keep going straight through its square before turning left or right in the next square. Ensure that this works for at least one route going into the port.

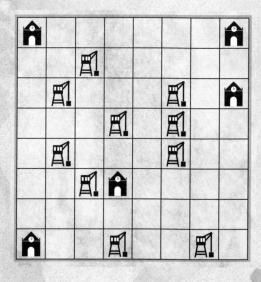

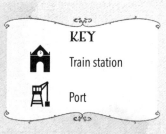

FOR SOLUTION SEE PAGE 222

NEUROTICS

You take a pit stop on a small island in the middle of the Pacific Ocean to stock up on supplies, and spend a couple of hours exploring the golden beaches that are teeming with unusual wildlife. Your new friend has also invited you to a dinner with a number of botanists and biologists who are currently researching the island's unique flora and fauna.

The conversation is stimulating, but after so long at sea with long stretches spent alone with your thoughts, you begin to find the conversation tricky to follow. You decide it is definitely time to call it a night when the woman next to you starts speaking and all you hear is a jumble of nonsensical words.

The following anagrams are things from all around the world. They have something in common and there is a clue in the title, which is also an anagram.

Can you unscramble the anagrams and discover what binds them together?

1.	**NEAR GIANT**
2.	**BOIL COMA**
3.	**CANDLES THUD**
4.	**SEE IT**
5.	**TRITE BARGAIN**
6.	**FERAL CAN**
7.	**INK PASTA**
8.	**A RUG PLOT**
9.	**GRIEVES**
10.	**DEFECATION TRAUMATISES**

REWARD

If you unscramble half the names, you win two green cards. Unveil all the names and you win three.

FOR SOLUTION SEE PAGE 223

WANDERING TO WONDERS

You devote just over a year to visiting the wonders of the world, which is well worth it in your opinion. Among the sights you see are:
• Machu Picchu – an Inca citadel near Cusco, Peru.
• The Great Wall of China.
• Yellowstone – the United States' famous National Park.
• Chichén Itzá – a Mayan city in Yucatán, Mexico.
• Petra – an ancient city in modern-day Jordan.

To record your exploits in your journal afterwards, you must recall which wonder you saw in which month, which method of transport you used to get to it and the prevailing weather on arrival.

Can you fill in all the facts from the clues below?
1. You were drenched by a rainstorm when you visited Yellowstone National Park.
2. The view on your donkey ride was obscured by a thick blanket of fog, but this was not during an excursion to a city.
3. You saw Petra during an odd-numbered month.
4. You were not travelling by camel during the blistering heatwave.
5. It snowed on Christmas Day.
6. The air was ominously still in January when you were somewhere in the Americas.
7. In October you took a boat to see a wonder, but it was not Chichén Itzá.
8. In April you headed to Peru and visited Machu Picchu.
9. You took a train to visit the Great Wall of China.

Month	Transport	Wonder	Weather
October			
January			
April			
July			
December			

	Camel	Train	Donkey	Boat	Hot air balloon	Machu Picchu	The Great Wall	Yellowstone	Chichén Itzá	Petra	Fog	Wind	Rainstorm	Snow	Heatwave
October															
January															
April															
July															
December															
Fog															
Wind															
Rainstorm															
Snow															
Heatwave															
Machu Picchu															
The Great Wall															
Yellowstone															
Chichén Itzá															
Petra															

REWARD
If get all the facts, you win three purple train cards.

FOR SOLUTION SEE PAGE 223

ALEXANDRIA TO CAIRO

Africa's rail network was founded in 1851 at the behest of Abbas I of Egypt, who commissioned the son of George Stephenson (the "Father of Railways") to build the continent's first standard gauge railway.

When you arrive in Egypt, you decide to retrace that first historic track. You must work out the route and insert the tracks into the grid opposite.

The numbers on the periphery tell you how many rail sections must be in that row or column, although unnumbered rows and columns may also have sections. You may place only a straight or a curved section inside a box. The tracks cannot cross themselves.

Straight

Curve

Can you connect Alexandria to Cairo?

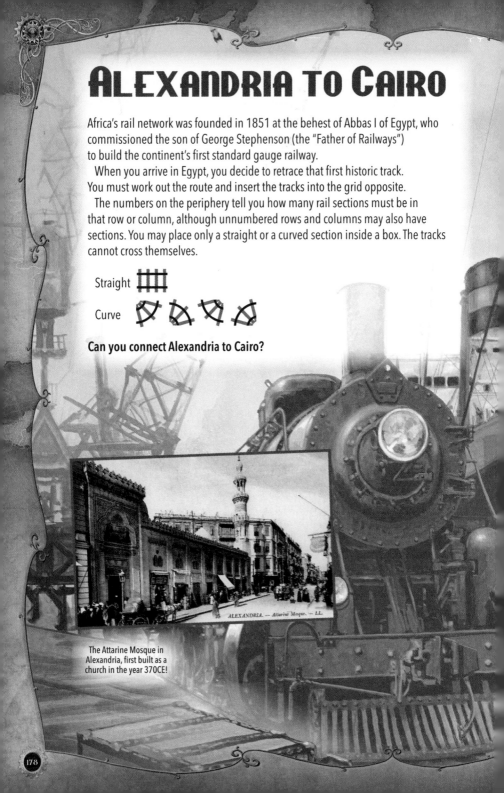

The Attarine Mosque in Alexandria, first built as a church in the year 370CE!

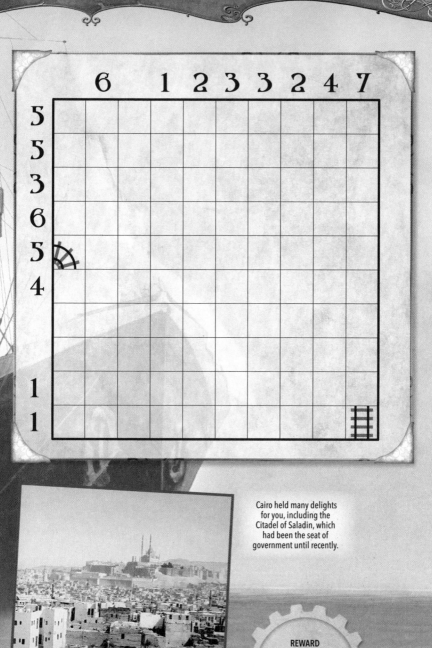

Cairo held many delights
for you, including the
Citadel of Saladin, which
had been the seat of
government until recently.

REWARD
If you connect
Alexandria to Cairo,
you win two multi-
coloured train cards.

FOR
SOLUTION
SEE PAGE
223

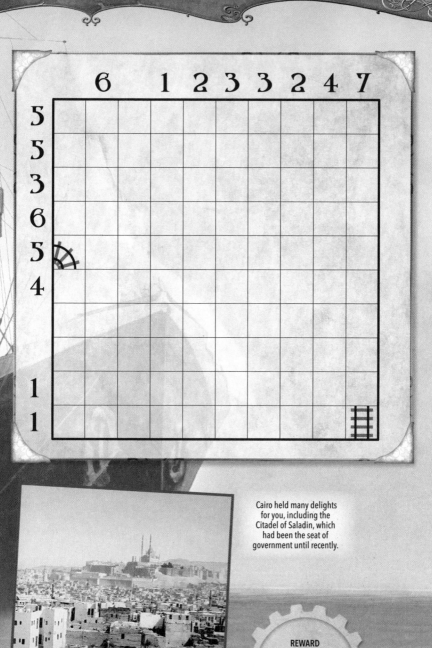
179

DAILY BREAD

In Eritrea, you receive a warm welcome and your host, Selassie, invites you to partake in a family tradition.

Once a week, Selassie bakes bread, then he takes the loaves to his elderly relatives before returning home for supper. His relatives live some distance apart, so he advises you to put on some sturdy walking shoes if you are not used to travelling barefoot. After so many rail journeys, a hike actually sounds quite appealing!

At each home, his relatives take half of the loaves he has brought, but always give him one back before he continues on his way. There are seven homes on Selassie's journey.

"It's a tradition because my relatives just like to have guests. They're perfectly capable of baking their own bread!" he says.

When you return to Selassie's house, you have just one loaf each for your supper.

How many loaves did Selassie bake?

REWARD
If you work it out, you win two white train cards.

FOR SOLUTION SEE PAGE 224

THE OUTBACK

On an adventurous impulse, you decide to journey into the Australian Outback – by bicycle! Don't worry, you are very proficient now.

   The weather is clear in the morning when you set off from Alice Springs for Barrow Creek. But after hours of peddling along the seemingly endless road, the sky suddenly turns black, and you are blasted by a thunderstorm.

   You cycle on heroically against the stinging wind, desperate to keep to the road. There is nowhere to take shelter in the wide-open country but, fortunately, there was not much lightning to worry about.

   The storm swiftly moves on and the blues skies return, but your relief is short-lived. You are in an uninhabited area and the storm has disorientated you.

   As you approach a junction in the road, your heart sinks yet further. The sturdy sign that you expected to see has been uprooted by the storm and thrown into a nearby ditch.

How will you find your way to Barrow Creek now?

REWARD
If you figure it out, you win one yellow train card.

FOR SOLUTION SEE PAGE 224

ISLAND HOPPING

French Polynesia is a group of beautiful and remote islands and atolls in the Pacific Ocean. You visit 20 of these idyllic getaways during your tour, but follow a circuitous route to do so.

  While sunning yourself on the Motutunga Atoll, your final destination and an uninhabited island with a vast lagoon that you are about to have a swim in, you decide to map out your journey.

Following the directions given beneath each island, where E is east, for example, and assuming you visited each location only once, can you work out where you started?

Rangiroa 3E	Takaroa 1S	Napuka 1S	Puka-Puka 2W
Kaukura 1S	Kauehi 2S	Takume 2W	Fangatau 3S
Fakarava 3E	Makemo 1E	Raroia 2S	Fakahina 1N
Tahanea 1S	Motutunga X	Hikueru 1E	Tatakoto 3W
Anaa 4N	Haraiki 2N	Hao 1N	Reao 2W

REWARD
If you figure
it out, you win
three black train
cards.

**FOR
SOLUTION
SEE PAGE
224**

EXCHANGE

Your tour is almost over, and during your travels you have acquired a significant amount of loose change in various foreign currencies. While on your final rail journey, you come across a money lender who offers to exchange a number of your coins for dollars, but his exchange rates seem unnecessarily cryptic.

Your wallet contains:

From the table opposite can you work out the dollar value of each of the four different types of coin and how much you will get for your four?

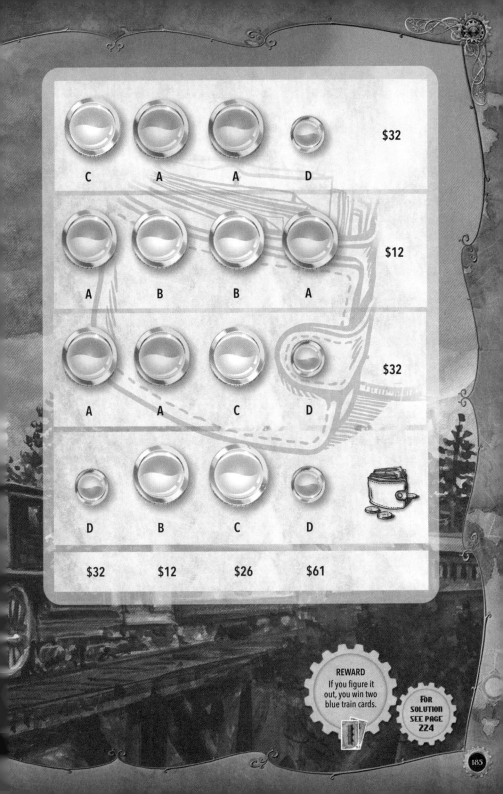

C   A   A   D $32

A   B   B   A $12

A   A   C   D $32

D   B   C   D

$32 $12 $26 $61

REWARD
If you figure it out, you win two blue train cards.

FOR SOLUTION SEE PAGE 224

Homeward Bound

The years have slipped away as you have circumnavigated the globe, and you finally feel worthy of the term "global traveller". Sadly, the moment has come for you to hang up your hiking boots and pack away your railway maps for the last time.

One of your final stops is the "lost city" of Petra, in Jordan. This magnificent ruined city is like nothing you have seen on the rest of your travels, and you can't think of a better way to end your adventure. To test your powers of observation one last time you have come up with a tricky visual task.

Two of the squares below are the correct squares that complete the puzzle, while the other ten of them have each been subtly altered.

Can you determine which two squares would correctly complete the image?

DID YOU KNOW?

Famous for its rock-cut architecture, Petra is one of the Seven New Wonders of the World. The ancient city was carved into the mountainside over 2,000 years ago and can only be accessed by walking through a narrow 1km-long gorge.

The ancient abandoned city of Petra in Jordan.

REWARD

If you identify the correct squares, you win four multi-coloured train cards. If you only identify one, you win two cards.

FOR SOLUTION SEE PAGE 224

THE SOLUTIONS

189

Pg. 10–11: Discover North America

1. Atlanta
2. Boston
3. Calgary
4. Charleston
5. Chicago
6. Dallas
7. Denver
8. Duluth
9. El Paso
10. Helena
11. Houston
12. Kansas City
13. Las Vegas
14. Little Rock
15. Los Angeles
16. Miami
17. Montreal
18. Nashville
19. New Orleans
20. New York
21. Oklahoma City
22. Omaha
23. Phoenix
24. Pittsburgh
25. Portland
26. Raleigh

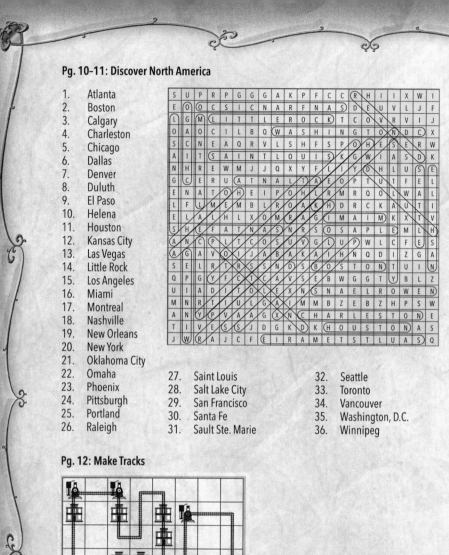

27. Saint Louis
28. Salt Lake City
29. San Francisco
30. Santa Fe
31. Sault Ste. Marie

32. Seattle
33. Toronto
34. Vancouver
35. Washington, D.C.
36. Winnipeg

Pg. 12: Make Tracks

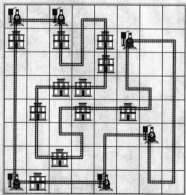

Pg. 13: Spare a Dime?

In a city like LA, street performing is highly competitive. Dougie's schtick has earned him notoriety, ensuring a steady flow of dimes from incredulous tourists.

Pg. 14–15: The Pioneers

Family	Year Est.	Business	Location
Stein	1890	Mining	Sacramento
Harvey	1891	Hotels	Denver
Brake	1892	Steel	Carson City
Graham	1893	Preaching	Fresno
McDonald	1894	Farming	Boise

Pg. 16–17: Connect the Midwest

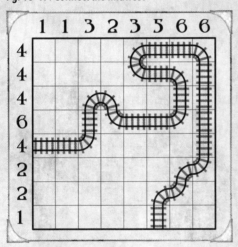

Pg. 18: Clay's Pigeon

A total of 225 miles. Travelling at 40 miles per hour, it will take Lucas 2½ hours to travel the 100 miles home. This means Betsy will be flying for 2½ hours at 90 miles per hour, so she will cover 225 miles.

Pg. 19: New York Minutes

Art and Bernie ride first, and with Bernie in charge this takes 2 minutes.
Bernie gets off and Art hurries back to the diner in 1 minute.
Charles and Donny head out next, taking 10 minutes, and both dismount.
Bernie rushes back to the diner, picks up Art and returns in a 4-minute round trip, just in time for the start of the game!

Pg. 20-21: The Big Apple

1. Brooklyn
2. Central Park
3. Chelsea
4. Chinatown
5. East Village
6. Empire State Building
7. Gramercy Park
8. Greenwich Village
9. Lincoln Center
10. Lower East Side
11. Midtown West
12. Soho
13. Times Square
14. United Nations
15. Wall Street

Pg. 22-23: Yuletide

The fourth and tenth carriages have been swapped. The code is based on a popular Christmas carol.

First	**PPT**	A Partridge in a Pear Tree
Second	**TTD**	Two Turtle Doves
Third	**TFH**	Three French Hens
Fourth	**FCB**	Four Calling Birds
Fifth	**FGR**	Five Gold Rings
Sixth	**SGL**	Six Geese a-Laying
Seventh	**SSS**	Seven Swans a-Swimming
Eighth	**EMM**	Eight Maids a-Milking
Ninth	**NLD**	Nine Ladies Dancing
Tenth	**TLL**	Ten Lords a-Leaping
Eleventh	**EPP**	Eleven Pipers Piping
Twelfth	**TDD**	Twelve Drummers Drumming

Pg. 24-25: All Change!

Pg. 28–29: Discover Europe

1. Angora
2. Athina
3. Barcelona
4. Brest
5. Brindisi
6. Bruxelles
7. Bucuresti
8. Budapest
9. Cádiz
10. Constantinople
11. Danzig
12. Dieppe
13. Edinburgh
14. Erzurum
15. Essen
16. Frankfurt
17. Kharkiv
18. København
19. Kyiv
20. Lisboa
21. London
22. Madrid
23. Marseille
24. Moskva
25. München
26. Palermo
27. Pamplona
28. Petrograd
29. Riga
30. Roma
31. Rostov
32. Sarajevo
33. Sevastopol
34. Smolensk
35. Smyrna
36. Sochi
37. Sofia
38. Stockholm
39. Venezia
40. Vilnius
41. Warszawa
42. Wien
43. Zagreb
44. Zurich

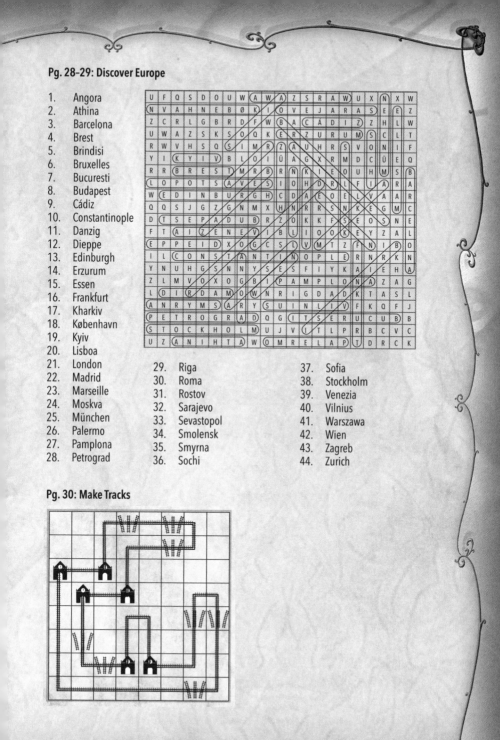

Pg. 30: Make Tracks

Pg. 31: Hastier Revery

1. Danube
2. Rhine
3. Rhone
4. Moselle
5. Loire
6. Dnieper
7. Thames
8. Tiber
9. Seine
10. Dordogne

The puzzle's title is an anagram of "They Are Rivers".

Pg. 32–33: The Orient Express

CARRIAGE	CAB	TENDER	1st CLASS	2nd CLASS	3rd CLASS
PASSENGER	MacDuff	Dupont	Romanova	Schmidt	Ozturk
PROFESSION	Driver	Fireman	Spy	Journalist	Artist
FROM	Istanbul	Strasburg	Varna	Bucharest	Budapest
TO	London	Calais	Paris	Munich	Vienna
DISTANCE	3,100 km	620 km	2,500 km	1,500 km	215 km

Pg. 34–35: Ottoman Empire

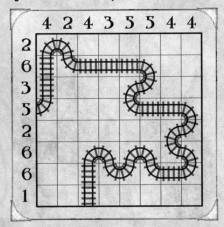

Pg. 36–37: Time Warp

The station's clock was a digital 24-hour clock! No wonder you were so confused. As far as you are aware, they haven't been invented yet. But then how can you be aware of something not yet invented… not worth thinking about. Each digit is created from seven lines and the second "hour" digit has a defect – the top right vertical line is unable to illuminate. So, when the clock showed 16:00, the true time was 18:00. When it was really 19:00, the clock showed 15:00. Had you waited until eight o'clock (20:00), the defect would have become apparent.

Pg. 38–39: Carriage Return

It will take 15 moves to reorder the carriages. An ➜ indicates that the carriage is pushed one space; A + on either side of a number indicates the carriage was lifted with a crane.

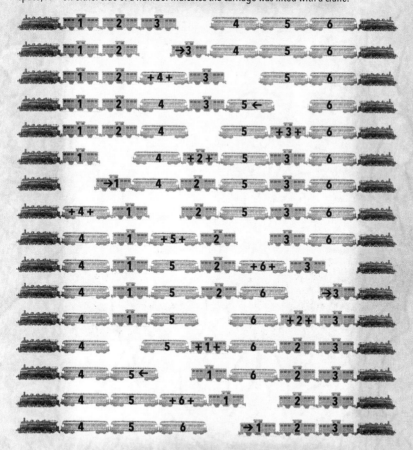

Pg. 40: Tongue-tied

	Hello	Goodbye	Thank you
Swedish	hallå	adjö	tack
Greek	χαίρετε	αντιο σας	ευχαριστώ
Lithuanian	sveiki	sudie	ačiū
Polish	dzień dobry	do widzenia	dziękuję ci
Portuguese	olá	tchau	obrigado

Pg. 41: Mythomania

You can ask either attendant the following question:

"If I asked your colleague which train I should take for Berlin, what would he say?"

Whatever answer you receive, take the opposite train and it will be the correct one.

Pg. 42–43: Jigsaw Jumble

Pg. 46–47: Discover Germany

1. Augsburg
2. Berlin
3. Bremen
4. Bremerhaven
5. Chemnitz
6. Dortmund
7. Dresden
8. Düsseldorf
9. Emden
10. Erfurt
11. Frankfurt
12. Freiburg
13. Hamburg
14. Hannover
15. Karlsruhe
16. Kassel
17. Kiel
18. Koblenz
19. Köln
20. Konstanz
21. Leipzig
22. Lindau
23. Magdeburg
24. Mainz
25. Mannheim
26. München
27. Münster
28. Nürnberg
29. Regensburg
30. Saarbrücken
31. Schwerin
32. Stuttgart
33. Ulm
34. Würzburg

Pg. 48: Make Tracks

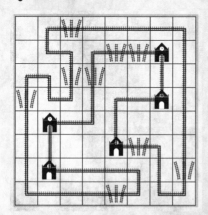

Pg. 49: Find Rank Dodo

1. Wiener Schnitzel — pan-fried breaded veal
2. Apfelkuchen — apple cake
3. Bratwurst — German sausage
4. Pumpernickel — heavy rye bread
5. Sauerkraut — fermented raw cabbage
6. Pilsner — the original pale lager
7. Kirschtorte — cherry cake
8. Riesling — white wine from the Rhine
9. Pretzel — twisted baked pastry
10. Gummibär — "gummy bears" sweets

"Find Rank Dodo" unscrambles to "Food and Drink".

Pg. 50-51: Oktoberfest

Guest	From	Number of sausages	Adventure
Heinz	Düsseldorf	5 sausages	Was sick
Birgit	Munich	6 sausages	Proposed
Hedwig	Cologne	12 sausages	Swam in canal
Otto	Berlin	10 sausages	Entered parade
Gustav	Ulm	8 sausages	Got lost

Pg. 52-53: Reunification

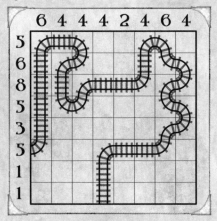

Pg. 54: Brocken Down

Monday. If you didn't fall into the trap of thinking "1,000m divided by a net daily gain of 100m equals 10 days," well done. The train actually reaches its destination by the evening of the eighth day.

	Day	Night
Mon	300m	100m
Tues	400m	200m
Weds	500m	300m
Thurs	600m	400m
Fri	700m	500m
Sat	800m	600m
Sun	900m	700m
Mon	1,000m	

Pg. 55: Excess Baggage

None. Don't be distracted by the percentages. If half of the 800 passengers have two items and the other half have none, it is the same as one item per passenger.

Pg. 56–57: Mysteries of the Illuminati

Alas, these are not arcane symbols, they are simply digital numbers and their mirror images, rotated 90 degrees anti-clockwise. Although what digital numbers are doing marked on the walls of early 20th century Munich does make you wonder… Did the Illuminati have something to do with that clock?

Pg. 58–59: Locomotion

	3	2	4	1	2	2	1	1	2	2	
6	🚂		🚂			🚃	🚂		🚃	🚂	6
0											0
2	🚂		🚂								2
0											0
4			🚃	🚃	🚃	🚂					4
0											0
0											0
8	🚃	🚃	🚂		🚃	🚂		🚃	🚃	🚂	8
0											0
0											0
	3	2	4	1	2	2	1	1	2	2	

Pg. 60–61: All Change!

Pg. 64–65: Discover France

1. Amiens
2. Angers
3. Avignon
4. Bayonne
5. Besançon
6. Bordeaux
7. Bourges
8. Brest
9. Briançon
10. Brive-la-Gaillarde
11. Calais
12. Cherbourg
13. Clermont-Ferrand
14. Dijon
15. Grenoble
16. La Rochelle
17. Le Havre
18. Le Mans
19. Lille
20. Limoges
21. Lorient
22. Lyon
23. Marseille
24. Metz
25. Montpellier
26. Mulhouse
27. Nancy
28. Nantes
29. Nice
30. Orléans
31. Paris
32. Pau
33. Perpignan
34. Poitiers
35. Reims
36. Rennes
37. Rodez
38. Rouen
39. Saint-Malo
40. Strasbourg
41. Toulouse
42. Tours

Pg. 66: Make Tracks

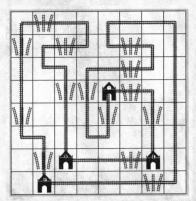

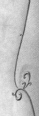

Pg. 67: Nasty Groom
1. Boeuf bourguignon
2. Baguette
3. Croissant
4. Crème brûlée
5. Macarons
6. Pain au chocolat
7. Soufflé
8. Foie gras
9. Camembert
10. Fromage frais

"Nasty Groom" is an anagram of "Gastronomy".

Pg. 68–69: Tour de France

Location	Food	Dessert	Month
Paris	Escargot	Macaron	March
Lyon	Coq au vin	Tarte tatin	May
Marseille	Boeuf bourguignon	Soufflé	April
Bordeaux	Croque monsieur	Fondant au chocolat	February
Nantes	Ratatouille	Profiteroles	June

Pg. 70–71: Brittany

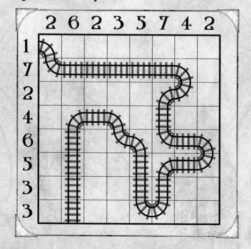

Pg. 72: Paris Match

R	I	S	A	P
P	A	R	I	S
A	R	P	S	I
I	S	A	P	R
S	P	I	R	A

Pg. 73: Eiffel Tower

It stands 324 meters tall, which is 162 meters plus half of 324 meters.

Pg. 74–75: Bordeaux

Tip the barrel until the water is just level with the rim, just at the point before it would spill out. Then look into the barrel: if you can see any part of the bottom, it is less than half-full; otherwise, it is more than half-full.

Pg. 76–77: Revolutions

Jacques was giving you a ride to the station on his bicycle. He arrived early and was able to stand in for the driver who had not showed up for work.

Pg. 78–79: Jigsaw Jumble

The other pieces of the jigsaw (A B C D F H I J K L) have all had the image of the palace and grounds moved around or reversed.

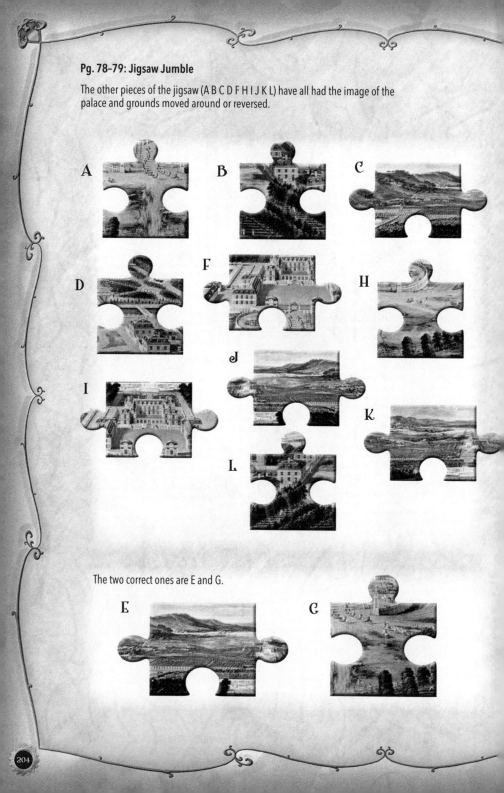

The two correct ones are E and G.

Pg. 82-83: Discover The Netherlands

1. Aarschot
2. Amsterdam
3. Antwerpen
4. Arnhem
5. Breda
6. Den Helder
7. Eindhoven
8. Emmen
9. Enschede
10. 's-Gravenhage
11. Groningen
12. Haarlem
13. Hasselt
14. 's-Hertogenbosch
15. Leeuwarden
16. Lelystad
17. Liège
18. Maastricht
19. Middelburg
20. Nijmegen
21. Roermond
22. Rotterdam
23. Sneek
24. Turnhout
25. Utrecht
26. Waddeneilanden
27. Zwolle

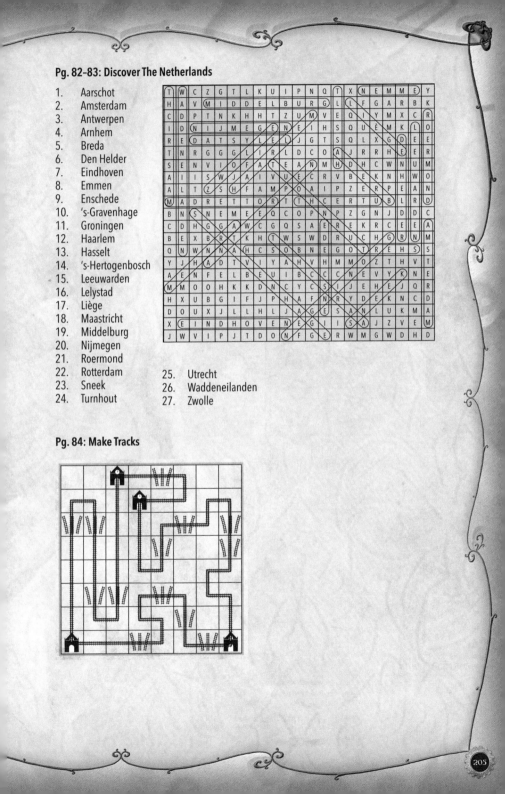

Pg. 84: Make Tracks

Pg. 85: A Fulsome Pope

1. Vincent van Gogh – post-Impressionist painter
2. William of Orange – Dutch monarch who later co-ruled England, Ireland and Scotland
3. Mata Hari – (stage name) dancer and First World War spy
4. Eddie Van Halen – US rock legend, born in Amsterdam
5. Queen Wilhelmina – monarch and world's first female dollar-billionaire
6. Johan Cruyff – football legend
7. Rutger Hauer – actor
8. Famke Janssen – actress
9. Jean-Claude van Damme – actor
10. Audrey Hepburn – actress

The words "A Fulsome Pope" unscramble to reveal "Famous People".

Pg. 86–87: Going Dutch

Day	Companion	Location	Activity
Monday	Elian	Zwolle	Windmills
Tuesday	Alex	Amsterdam	Tulips
Wednesday	Beau	Groningen	Clogs
Thursday	Dani	Haarlem	Cheese shop
Friday	Chris	Rotterdam	Canal trip

Pg. 88–89: Rotterdam to Amsterdam

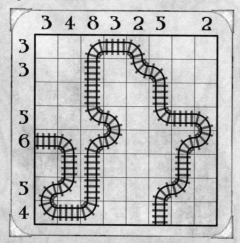

Pg. 90–91: Mondrian-esque
The colours move clockwise through the squares and the entire picture is rotated 90 degrees clockwise each time.

Pg. 92–93: Return Ticket
Yes. If you imagine a train coming back from Brussels around the same time as your outbound journey, there would always be a point where you pass one another.

Pg. 94: Polders

Pg. 95: Windmills

Pg. 96-97: All Change!

Pg. 100–101: Discover Italy

1. Agrigento
2. Ancona
3. Bari
4. Bergamo
5. Bologna
6. Bolzano
7. Cagliari
8. Catania
9. Cosenza
10. Firenze
11. Foggia
12. Genova
13. Grosseto
14. Lecce
15. Messina
16. Milano
17. Napoli
18. Olbia
19. Palermo
20. Parma
21. Perugia
22. Pescara
23. Pisa
24. Roma
25. Salerno
26. Sassari
27. Siracusa
28. Taranto
29. Tarvisio
30. Torino
31. Trieste
32. Venezia
33. Verona

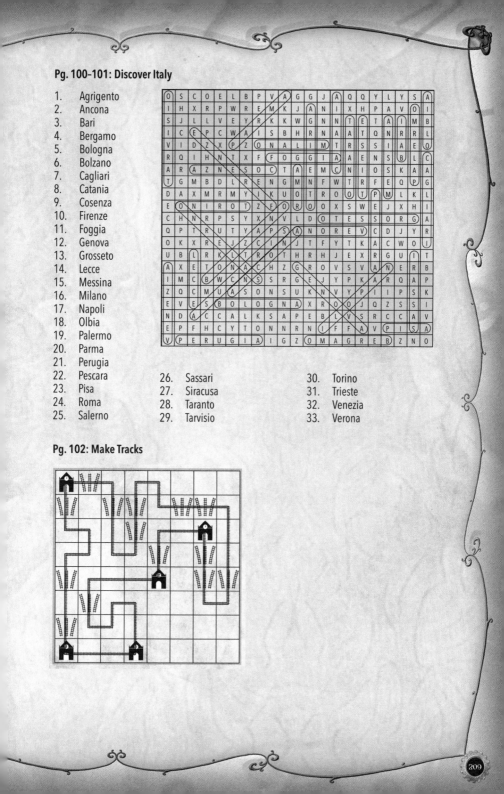

Pg. 102: Make Tracks

Pg. 103: Sad Abs Unform

1. Alfa Romeo
2. Dolce and Gabbana
3. Ferrari
4. Giorgio Armani
5. Lamborghini
6. Martini
7. Maserati
8. Peroni
9. Pirelli
10. Prada
11. Versace

The title "Sad Abs Unform" is an anagram of "Famous Brands".

Pg. 104–105: Mysteries of the Tarot

You know that there are three ranks: King, Queen and Knight, and three suits: Cups, Swords and Wands. First try to work out the order of the suits:

Clue 1	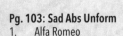	the Cup must be to the left of the Sword, however…
Clue 4		the Sword must be to the right of the Wand, however…
Clue 3		the Wand must be to the right of the King.

KING of CUPS.

KNIGHT of WANDS.

QUEEN of SWORDS.

Now you know the order of suits and you also know that the King is Cups (clue 3), so you can conclude from clue 2 that the Knight is Wands and that the Queen is Swords.

Pg. 106–107: Verona to Venice

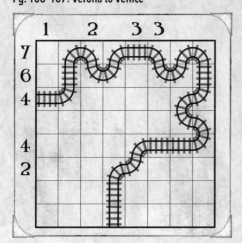

Pg. 108: Pisa

The missing letter is o. The first sequence is the initial letters of cardinal numbers 0 to 8 in Italian.

0	1	2	3	4	5	6	7	8
zero	uno	due	tre	quattro	cinque	sei	sette	otto

The second is the Fibonacci sequence in which the next number is derived by adding together the two numbers preceding it.

0	1	1	2	3	5	8
zero	uno	uno	due	tre	cinque	otto

Fibonacci is Leonardo Bonacci's widely known sobriquet.

Pg. 109: Five to Four

English. If you remove the first and last letter from the word FIVE, you get IV. This is the Roman numeral for 4.

Pg. 110–111: Tuscany

The return journey was slightly faster.
$1/50 + 1/66 = 0.03515$, which is greater than $2/57 = 0.03508$.

Pg. 112–113: Renaissance Graffiti

The numbers are: 14, 13, 1, 3, 8, 9, 1, 22, 5, 12, 12, 9
Which, if you use a straightforward alphanumeric substitution code (A = 1, B = 2, etc.)
reveals:

NMACHIAVELLI

Niccolò Machiavelli was a sixteenth-century diplomat and political
writer, whose name is now synonymous with intrigue and
cynicism. He wasn't particularly popular with the Church.

Pg. 114–115: Jigsaw Jumble

Pg. 118–119: Discover the British Isles

1. Aberdeen
2. Aberystwyth
3. Belfast
4. Birmingham
5. Brighton
6. Bristol
7. Cambridge
8. Cardiff
9. Carlisle
10. Cork
11. Dover
12. Dublin
13. Dundalk
14. Dundee
15. Edinburgh
16. Fort William
17. Galway
18. Glasgow
19. Holyhead
20. Hull
21. Inverness
22. Ipswich
23. Leeds
24. Limerick
25. Liverpool
26. Llandrindod Wells
27. London
28. Manchester
29. Newcastle
30. Northampton
31. Norwich
32. Nottingham
33. Penzance
34. Plymouth
35. Reading
36. Sligo
37. Southampton
38. Stornoway
39. Stranraer
40. Tullamore
41. Ullapool
42. Wick

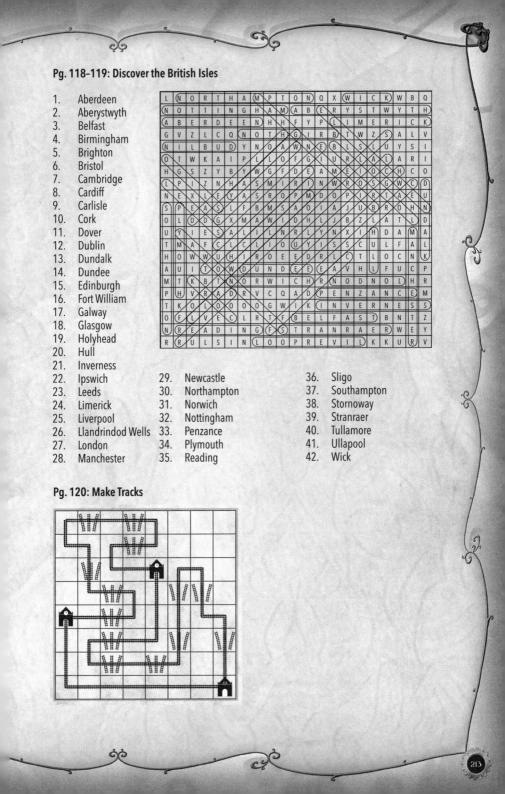

Pg. 120: Make Tracks

Pg. 121: After Our Swims

1. Arthur Conan Doyle
2. Charles Dickens
3. Ian Fleming
4. JK Rowling
5. George Orwell
6. Virginia Woolf
7. Jane Austen
8. Roald Dahl
9. Oscar Wilde
10. Maeve Binchy

"After Our Swims" is an anagram of "Famous Writers".

Pg. 122–123: A Week in London

Day	Site	Bought	Transport
Monday	Regent's Park	Fish and chips	Bicycle
Tuesday	Nelson's Column	Cup of tea	Walk
Wednesday	Madame Tussaud's	Flag	Underground
Thursday	Big Ben	Book	Bus
Friday	V & A Museum	Map	Hackney carriage

Pg. 124–125: Race to the North

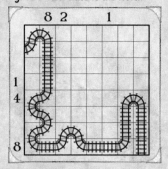

Pg. 126–127: Not a Poem

At the end of the se(a)	A						
the first person (of the verb) to be	A	M					
angry or crazy	M	A	D				
contrived	M	A	D	E			
a fantasy	D	R	E	A	M		
you hold them in high esteem	A	D	M	I	R	E	
but have judged them wrongly	M	I	S	R	E	A	D
the merrows!	M	E	R	M	A	I	D	S

Pg. 128: Painting by numbers

The third row (21–30), which has 17 of the letter E. The ninth row (81–90) has 18 and the tenth (91–100) has 19.

Pg. 129: What's Occurin'?

The total number of occurrences of the number 1 is: 3
The total number of occurrences of the number 2 is: 2
The total number of occurrences of the number 3 is: 3
The total number of occurrences of the number 4 is: 1
The total number of occurrences of the number 5 is: 1

Pg. 130–131: Locomotion

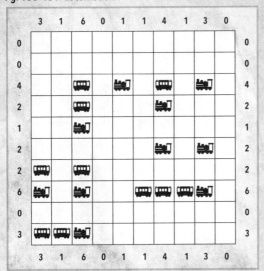

	3	1	6	0	1	1	4	1	3	0	
0											0
0											0
4			🚃		🚂		🚃		🚂		4
2			🚃				🚂				2
1			🚂								1
2							🚂		🚂		2
2	🚃		🚃								2
6	🚂		🚂			🚃	🚃	🚃	🚂		6
0											0
3	🚃	🚃	🚂								3
	3	1	6	0	1	1	4	1	3	0	

Pg. 132–133: All Change!

Pg. 136–137: Discover Scandinavia

1. Ålborg
2. Åndalsnes
3. Århus
4. Bergen
5. Boden
6. Göteborg
7. Helsinki
8. Honningsvåg
9. Imatra
10. Kajaani
11. Karlskrona
12. Kirkenes
13. Kiruna
14. København
15. Kristiansand
16. Kuopio
17. Lahti
18. Lillehammer
19. Mo i Rana
20. Narvik
21. Norrköping
22. Örebro
23. Oslo
24. Östersund
25. Rovaniemi
26. Stavanger
27. Stockholm
28. Sundsvall
29. Tallinn
30. Tampere
31. Tornio
32. Tromsø
33. Trondheim
34. Turku
35. Umeå
36. Vaasa

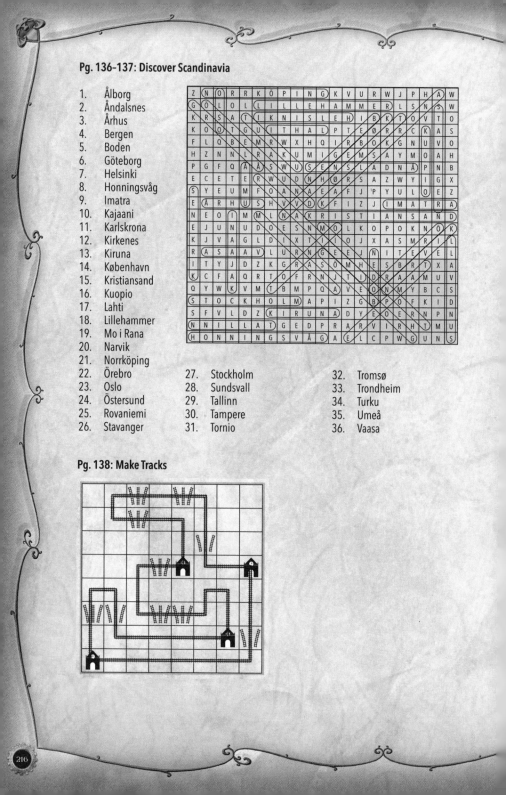

Pg. 138: Make Tracks

Pg. 139: Cast Code Snares Rats

1. Alicia Vikander
2. Max von Sydow
3. Stellan Skarsgård
4. Mads Mikkelsen
5. Nikolaj Coster-Waldau
6. Noomi Rapace
7. Ingrid Bergman
8. Greta Garbo
9. Rebecca Ferguson
10. Britt Ekland

The clue, "Cast Code Snares Rats", rearranges to "Actors and Actresses".

Pg. 140-141: Wildlife

Month	Location	Guide	Animal
February	Norway	Elisabet	Musk Ox
April	Sweden	Britta	Wolverine
June	Denmark	Anna	Brown Bear
August	Finland	Cecilia	Eagle
October	Iceland	Dagmar	Arctic Fox

Pg. 142-143: Copenhagen to Gothenburg

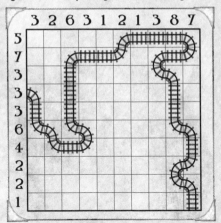

Pg. 144-145: Flags

		SE			FI
	DK		SE	DK	
		FI	NO		
NO		FI	FI		
SE	DK	SE	NO		
NO				DK	

Pg. 146–147: Nature Trail
You start at B3.

Pg. 148: Midsummer
Erik's family tree is complicated with cousins intermarrying – a common enough practice in the 19th century. The four relations at the table are one and the same person: Carl!

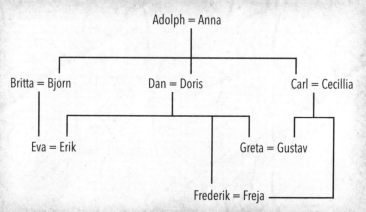

Adolph = Anna

Britta = Bjorn   Dan = Doris   Carl = Cecillia

Eva = Erik   Greta = Gustav

Frederik = Freja

This puzzle has been modified from Lewis Carroll's *A Tangled Tale*.

Pg. 149: Passage of Time
She is telling the truth if the date of your conversation is 1st January and Akka's birthday falls on New Year's Eve. This means that she was 97 two days ago, turned 98 on 31st December last year and will be 99 on the same date this year, so next year she will be 100.

Pg. 150–151: All Change!

Pg. 154–155: Discover Asia

1. Agra
2. Ankara
3. Astrakhan
4. Bangkok
5. Bombay
6. Calcutta
7. Chita
8. Colombo
9. Dihua
10. Hanoi
11. Irkutsk
12. Karachi
13. Kathmandu
14. Khabarovsk
15. Kobe
16. Krasnoyarsk
17. Lhasa
18. Macau
19. Mandalay
20. Mecca
21. Moscow
22. Omsk
23. Peking
24. Perm
25. Rangoon
26. Rawalpindi
27. Saigon
28. Samarkand
29. Seoul
30. Shanghai
31. Shiraz
32. Singapore
33. Taipei
34. Tbilisi
35. Tehran
36. Ulan Bator
37. Vladivostok
38. Xian

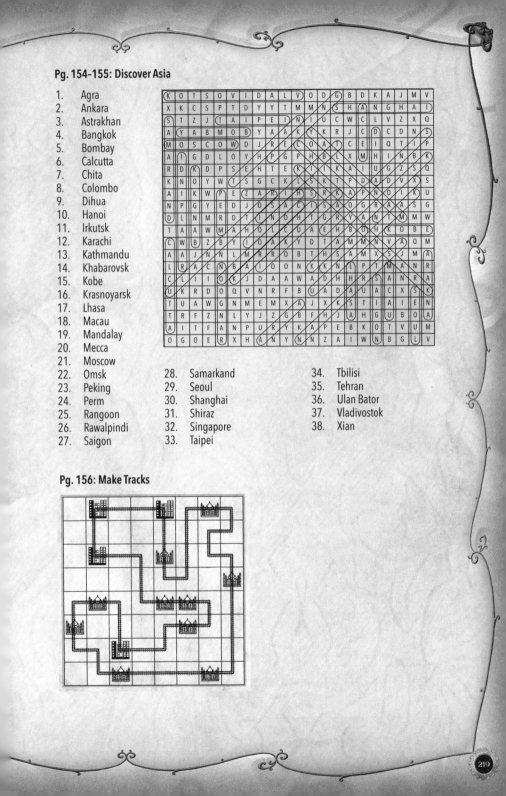

Pg. 156: Make Tracks

Pg. 157: A Jar Spawned No Sole

1. Anime
2. Futon
3. Karaoke
4. Karate
5. Origami
6. Samurai
7. Shiatsu
8. Teriyaki
9. Tsunami

The title "A Jar Spawned No Sole" translates to "Japanese Loanwords". You are currently in the region around Kobe.

Pg. 158–159: Take your seat

You were in seat number 5.

ENGINE	Nikita	Victor	Oleg	Tatiana	YOU	Yelena	Boris	Sofia

Pg. 160–161: Trans-Siberia

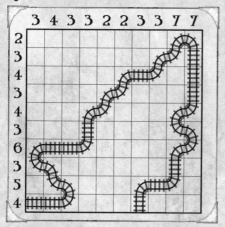

Pg. 162–163: Arabic Numerals

Swap the blue carriage numbers, but turn the 9 upside down so it becomes a 6. Then both trains will add up to 18.

Pg. 164: A Dream of Things to Come

4	2	3	5	7	9	6	1	8
8	1	6	3	4	2	7	5	9
7	5	9	8	6	1	4	3	2
1	9	8	7	3	6	2	4	5
2	6	4	1	5	8	3	9	7
5	3	7	2	9	4	8	6	1
9	8	5	6	2	3	1	7	4
6	7	1	4	8	5	9	2	3
3	4	2	9	1	7	5	8	6

Pg. 165: Technology

They are all timepieces: a sundial, a sand timer, a mechanical watch and a digital clock (probably a prototype).

Pg. 166–167: Locomotion

	0	4	1	3	1	4	1	4	2	0	
6		🚃		🚃		🚃	🚃	🚃	🚂		6
2		🚃		🚃							2
2		🚂		🚂							2
2						🚂		🚂			2
0											0
2						🚂		🚂			2
0											0
6		🚃	🚂		🚃	🚂		🚃	🚂		6
0											0
0											0
	0	4	1	3	1	4	1	4	2	0	

Pg. 168–169: All Change!

Pg. 172–173: Discover the World

1. Al-Qahira
2. Anchorage
3. Athína
4. Bangkok
5. Beijing
6. Buenos Aires
7. Cambridge Bay
8. Cape Town
9. Caracas
10. Casablanca
11. Christchurch
12. Dar Es Salaam
13. Darwin
14. Djibouti
15. Edinburgh
16. Hamburg
17. Hong Kong
18. Honolulu
19. Jakarta
20. Lagos
21. Lahore
22. Lima
23. Los Angeles
24. Luanda
25. Manila
26. Marseille
27. Miami
28. Moskva

29. Mumbai
30. New York
31. Novosibirsk
32. Perth
33. Port Moresby
34. Reykjavik
35. Rio de Janeiro
36. Sydney

37. Tehran
38. Tiksi
39. Toamasina
40. Tokyo
41. Valparaíso
42. Vancouver

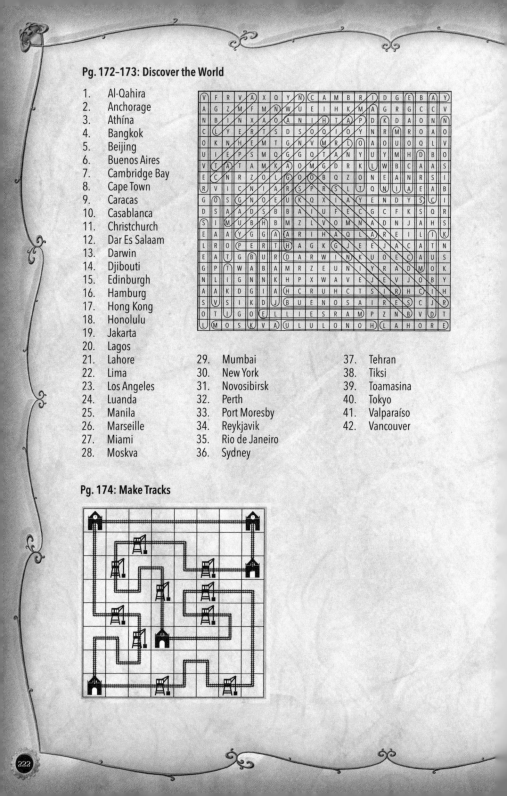

Pg. 174: Make Tracks

Pg. 175: Neurotics

1. Argentina
2. Colombia
3. Deutschland (Germany)
4. Eesti (Estonia)
5. Great Britain
6. La France
7. Pakistan
8. Portugal
9. Sverige (Sweden)
10. United States of America

The word "Neurotics" rearranges to "Countries".

Pg. 176–177: Wandering to Wonders

Month	Transport	Wonder	Weather
October	Boat	Yellowstone	Rainstorm
January	Hot air balloon	Chichén Itzá	Heatwave
April	Donkey	Machu Picchu	Fog
July	Camel	Petra	Wind
December	Train	The Great Wall	Snow

Pg. 178–179: Alexandria to Cairo

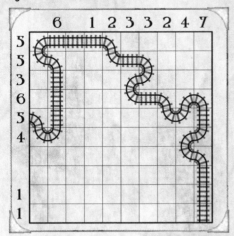

Pg. 180: Daily Bread
Two! At each home he gives away half of his loaves (one loaf) and receives the same number of loaves back.

Pg. 181: The Outback
If you can retrieve the sign and put it back into its hole with the arrow for Alice Springs pointing in the direction you came from, the other arrows will point to their true destinations.

Pg. 182-183: Island Hopping
You started your trip on Napuka.

Pg. 184-185: Exchange
You will get $55 for your coins.

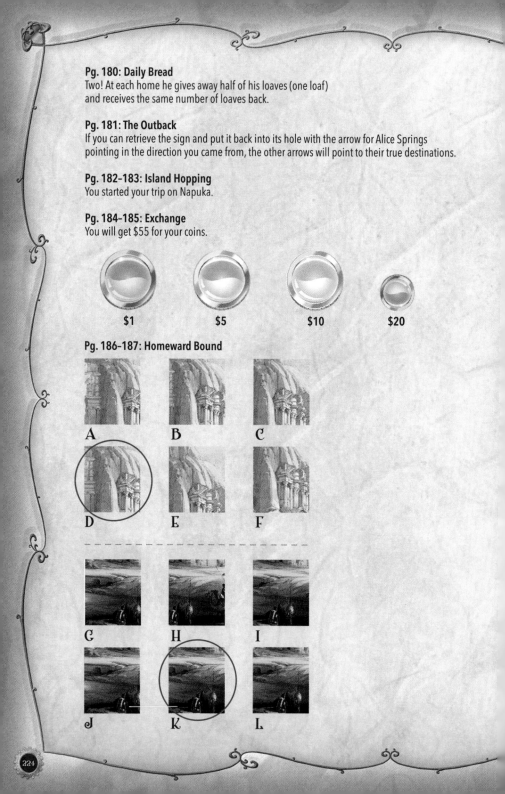

$1 $5 $10 $20

Pg. 186-187: Homeward Bound

A B C
D E F

G H I
J K L